HEADONISM

HEADONISM

PETER HEAD
WITH MJ CORNWALL

Copyright 2025 Peter Head

Printed by BookPOD

This book is copyright. Apart from any use permitted under the Copyright Act 1968 and subsequent amendments, no part may be reproduced, stored in a retrieval system or transmitted by any means or process whatsoever without written permission.

Enquiries about this publication can be made to the author via email: mctoons@bigpond.net.au

First published 2025

ISBN: 978-0-6454923-4-7 (paperback)
ISBN: 978-0-6454923-5-4 (e-book)

Cover art: Louise Cornwall
Front cover photo: Katerina Stratos

Head, Peter 1946-
Cornwall, Mark 1957-
Head, Peter, 1946- Biography
Entertainment- Australia- History
Music- Australia- History

 A catalogue record for this book is available from the National Library of Australia

For Mouse, Josh and Jac, Lo and Aden, Dutch and Chester and Holiday.

Hope you get a laugh out of it.

I do not have time to become famous or get rich.

-Vytas Serelis

NOTE

This story contains vernacular from times bygone, pertaining to gender, sexuality, cultural background and related aspects.

We beg the reader's leave that such is used here for no reason other than to portray attitudes and culture as they were, for insight into those times.

There are also allusions in the text to predatory sexual behaviours and related practices.

These are not intended in any way to encourage, enable or normalise such conduct, nor offer agency for apologists, only a full and frank picture of the way it was.

This story also contains the names of Indigenous people who have died.

FOREWORD

I love this for the strong, steeped South Australian tang and twang of the early chapters. You other Australians couldn't possibly taste it like we do. Also, buried there in the compacted, rich, loamy text is this description of the young apprentice plumber and singer Johnny Farnham as 'it's like Billy Eckstine fucked Wayne Newton.'

Music lover, I challenge you not to read on!

Dave Graney

PROLOGUE

In a car, alone, said Vince when he called with that worst of bad news. Same as Hank Williams had.

'I just want to let you know,' I said. 'A friend of mine.' The chatter stopped dead when I said the name. 'Sorry. I can't play any more tonight.' The Alice, its Riverside Hotel, as odd a place as any to be hit with such tidings.

On foot, bound for the bank of the Todd, I saw I was being followed. Everyone from the gig. And another thing. *Cops. Blackfellas. Walking together.*

Only Bon could do that.

'Geezus, Peter.' All along the river, yarns going round. Stories of Bon, and most of them true. 'I've had a word to the others,' said the only cop I ever called a friend. Me, too dazed to register. 'What I mean is,' he said, 'you, the mob, can drink down here, smoke some dope. Just for tonight. We didn't see it.'

Get this, Bon, I pictured myself writing, as he would have. *I'm in the Alice. Yeah, yet another piano bar. PhoneHead told me. We're having a wake for you. The whatnots, as you call them, say we're off the chain. Just for you, Lofty...*

ONE

It was wartime, when every night on earth could be your last. A party, at this mansion, some grazier dynasty in the Adelaide Hills. The courting, swift and furtive as the ghosts of Peramangk and Kaurna massacres hereabouts peered in through its hundred windows.

An RAAF pilot was TJ, or 'Tim', of clan McKellar. Maybe explains my distaste for bagpipes, tartan, cold countries. A dasher, TJ. And a bolter. Pat, fed fibs of his end in a training mishap when she called the base with the news. Yep. Born a bastard, me. And sired by one. And he was a piano player. And I'm still both. January 1946, made my entrance, all kick and wail. I'd see no more of Pat for some time.

Kilkenny lies west of the Torrens river, that glorified creek that cleaves Adelaide in twain. Port Road, straight up the guts of the west. Along the way, this burb, a name plucked from Ireland, a resemblance less than zero.

'You can always pick the dagoes.' Another charming word for *wogs*, migrants fresh off the post-war ships. Their front yards here, vegetable plots. *Dagoes*. Kids picked it up from their olds, flung it at them for sport, but these *New Australians* had known famine. Way ahead of the game.

My blood mob, their yards, plaster brolgas or roos. Or the odd blackfella, standing on one leg, mute monuments a la chintz to slaughters of which we knew nothing. The Italians, fearless and defiant, painted their homes in electric blue and stripper pink.

My kind of people.

Len and Lorna, names that could badge a folk music duo or a plate-spinning act, my adoptive parents. A sibling of their procreation, Robert, made the scene two years on from me. We were the Beagleys. Len drove a truck for a quid, for the Commonwealth Steel Company. Lorna, a stay at home parent as they say now. And seminal influencer. Hipped me to those magic faraway lands, music and the movies.

School. At Challa Gardens Primary, a failed Australian. That day I first played footy, I tried and died. A correlating horror for the mulga, the bush, abides. Len tried to straighten me out. Took me to see his team West Torrens, the Blood 'n' Tars, play Port Adelaide. Robert, a natural at footy. Genes. I didn't get the ones he did.

'Who wants to see the Hell Drivers?' And Len loved Rowley Park Speedway, its stock cars, hot rods. Me too, back then. Not now. Not my kind of music.

'That is correct, Beagley. The rest of you, wake up Australia!' My birth parents must have had it upstairs. I'd answer the first Q at the start of class, so the teachers would leave me be. But Aussie kids, not big on smartarses. So I confected a bodgie me, moves copped from the mean kids in my orbit. High school, went all the way Elvis, then crossed over to the full Jerry Lee. Damned and doomed.

Most kids here, no taste for schoolwork. They'd bail at fifteen, to bundy on at the GMH assembly line, the Clipsal factory at Bowden, the John Shearer plant in Kilkenny, or the Coca Cola setup near the old Adelaide Gaol. In the ghostpast of the Colony, once were public hangings there.

There were swarms of 'em. Italians, Greeks, and the *Balts*, the olds called them. Latvians, Lithuanians, Estonians, Poles. Often as not, smart as a camel-hair coat, but the classes were all in English, so some stumbled, or folded their hand and zoned out. Teachers cursed them as dim and dense. Factory fodder. So who cares?

'What a friend we have in Jesus...' Lorna was of the Congregational church. Not devout by any stretch, yet her mum insisted Robert and I go to Congo Sunday school, for righteous road maps. I dug the tales of talking serpents, great floods, severed heads on platters.

Then along came showbiz.

'Gotta see a man about a dog.' Sundays, Len would take off in his truck. Rolled back with cartons of longnecks or steel cans, for a party in the garage with rellos and the *reffos* from down the road. The frosties, filched from a depot, most like. As racist as most, Len. But he liked having the Italians over. 'They make good red plonk.'

My showie within was stirred awake when Lorna made me some hand puppets and I devised shows for the Sunday boozers' kids. My stage, our flat-roofed chookhouse behind the garage, next to the cocky's cage. I crouched behind it as my two fistfuls flounced and fought their way through short, brutal scripts.

Lorna, hipper than most. Radio never off, cat's whisker dial to a music station. Up and down our streets, other sounds. Barking mongrels, bodgies revving hotted-up early model Fords or Holdens, now and then, imported Pontiacs, Studebakers. Or the *ffsst!* of red or green scab ripped from a longneck of Southwark or West End, as fifty thousand battlers who looked like Jackie Gleason drained them till they felt no pain.

'Like that lucky old sun, give me nothin' to do...' From Lorna's cream and green wireless, I grew a garden of sonic muscle memories. Frankie Laine, Dinah Shore, Nat King Cole's *Mona Lisa* or The Platters, *The Great Pretender*. *'I seem to be, What I'm not, you see.'* Yeah, well. If ever a line sploshed up a painting of showbiz.

The Scream comes to mind.

'Get a shuffle on, boys. We'll miss the cartoons.' Saturdays, the flicks. *Jedda, Forbidden Planet, The Girl Can't Help It.* That last one, my first rock'n' roll joyride, Little Richard, Gene Vincent, Eddie Cochran on the rip and burn.

Once, a live show at Memorial Drive, to gawp in wonder at these vocal groups from beyond the sea, from *America*, The Inkspots, the Platters and, wait for it, the Harlem Globetrotters. I'd never seen black people till now, let alone seen them sing. The Globetrotters, a pro basketball team. Played it for laughs as they ran rings of fire round these white trash local players. I alone laughing out loud.

Few days later, at the shack we rented at West Beach for our annual sun and surf holiday, I see the Globetrotters, out on the porch about six up from ours. Their billet while in town, they told me, happy to pass the time with a pale kid from a strange land. I took to passing by every day just so I could hang, catch their stories from that mad world of travelling entertainers. Seemed, even then, I could love that life well.

'Just for fun. Like Luna Park,' he said. This, Len's ancient wooden flute he'd break out and play when he had a few beers on board. I kept going to the drawer for that tootstick, reefing it out for a blow. Seven by then, so old enough to stick up my hand when they asked.

Same as all such, our primary school band. All, including this rookie fife player, out of tune with each other, and the *squawk* of bum notes from young fingers, yet all on the same fantastic voyage.
Like jazz.

'You're a switched-on lad, boy.' Just like that. Me, the new bandleader, anointed by our bandmaster, who swung by the school once a week. I'd become so over and again, across the decades, that heavy crown of a snakes and ladders deal with the devil.

Yeah, being in a band. *Made me feel good about myself.* A uniform, navy blue strides and ties, white bandsman's belt, grey shirt. Back in that long ago, the wardrobe of war heroes.

Even cooler threads at my next gig, the Adelaide Fife And Drum Band. Blazing red jacket, gold braid and epaulettes. And an *audience*, for this be a *marching* band, parades through the CBD, the Square Mile they called it, for the John Martins' Xmas Pageant, or those martial cavalcades of which Menzies' Australia was so fond.

Yet I grew restless. *There's more to life than fife.*

As west as it gets from here, shoreside Indian Ocean, a boy my age, playing drums in a Highland pipe band. Ronald Belford Scott would drop into my life down the line. Now *that* was a time.

TWO

'This is middle C,' she said. *Gling*. 'The signpost to everything.' Our Auntie Chris had an old Beale upright. Whenever we paid a call, I'd beeline it for this music box, ping away at it, nut out pop songs by ear.

'Happy birthday, Peter.' The day I turned ten, it sailed to ours aboard Len's truck. *The beast was mine.* My eighty-eight keys to the Kingdom.

'Every Good Boy Deserves Fruit,' she said, peering down at me alongside her on the bench. 'Listening, Peter? *EGBDF.*' Mrs Chappell schooled me in the voodoo of stave and clefs, *Fur Elise,* that rookie rite of passage, and mush from the hit parade, fairy floss like *Tammy,* the Debbie Reynolds thing, or *Round The World*. Sonic baby food. Corny? *Off the cob, man*. But then, something wild. She never jerried, and I never told her what lay grinning within the boogie woogie bass of *Roll Out The Barrel.*

Within my soul now, the devil's left hand.

'*...lies a body, oozing life...*' Mindmapping on my piano, off the wireless, Pops Armstrong's *Mack The Knife,* Tennessee Ernie Ford's *Sixteen Tons.* Yeah, I strayed. Sight reading the only ship to sail in Mrs Chappell's lessons, and here's me, flying by the seat of my ears. Groovin', on a Sunday afternoon.

'How about the *Go-Boys*? I had a piano, so Robert scored a gift too right about now, a Ludwig like Ringo's. The puppet shows for Sunday's tipsy grownups punted now for our brother act. An out of town tryout. Way out of town.

'There it is!' That last year of primary school, October, the Russians launched the first radio satellite, Sputnik I. You could just see it, crossing under the stars, a thing of wonder. Got me musing on a bigger cosmic picture, on the odds of alien life, piqued by fuzzy pix of *flying saucers* in those bawdy mags like *Australasian Post* you'd flick through at the barber's.

It was about now I concluded that God as origin story didn't cut it. But *this*...

Meanwhile, down on the ground, our PM For Life, Bob Menzies, prophesied that the USSR and Red China meant us harm. It was all the talk among the adults.

'They'll do what the Japs tried to. My word they will. For our wool, our wheat. Our *coal*.'

Khruschev and Mao raved of nothing else, it seemed. To doubt it, well. *Unaustralian*.

THREE

Come 1958, year one, Woodville High. Here, a sea of strangers, eyes like wreckers' yard dogs. Some, it was plain, out to kill you if they could.

And something else. One day, here I be, seeing the girls in our class in a whole new way, that reflexive disdain vanished and instead an urge within to turn their heads from the footy stars and roughnuts here who had them entranced. How, well, soon came, as an angel with a sword of fire, via the rock 'n' roll on 5AD, *1310 on the dial*.

'You could make a good living playing this gear.' A nod of bodgie approval from classmates to this, but they didn't share my daydream. To them, the factories hereabouts, wonderlands, dispensing sacks of gold for the utopian idyll these would buy. The sag of the faces of their dads, the purpleblack eyes and split lips their mums wore, foretold otherwise. Or they'd rhapsodise of futures as builder's labourers, or at Windsor Chickens, a poultry slaughterhub right in the blue heart of the city. Pure Adelaide, that one.

Always was an Eraserhead kind of town.

Those first years at Woody, I made the top stream, the brainiacs. But in the end, it never had a prayer up against the might of heart's desire. Some teachers, ratshit, but not Mr Phillips and Mr Narroway. *Theatrical types*, the olds called them.

'His men *loved* each other.' Mr Phillips, on what spurred Alexander The Great's gory chain of victories and plunder. And Narroway sold us more Wilde than we'd ever need. To him, old Oscar *the* greatest ever, no contest, over Shakespeare, Hemingway, Woolf, the Brontes, Dickens, all comers.

'Just take it home, dear boy. Someone might as well put it to good use.' Mr Phillips had gleaned that I was a pianist and aspiring recording artiste. The school had a high-end reel to reel tape deck. 'You record *here*, listen back to your piece *here*.' He smiled. '*Alrrriiight?*'

He let me keep it at home for weeks on end. He was no predator. That deck, our only dirty secret. And he saw where I was headed, long before any other.

FOUR

'*When the band slows down we'll yell for more...*' A head like a butcher's dog, but this mutt ripped out of the radio like a sack of snakes dropped on hot tin. And easy as EAB. Three chords, no waiting. I looked both ways, saw no cops, and jumped on that train.

But Haley and his Comets, soon eclipsed by others, both piano players, *like me*. My first records, 78 RPM monsters, the sound of hell escaped and on the run. Double A sides, the Georgia Peach, Little Richard's *Long Tall Sally*, flip, *Tutti Frutti*. The other, Jerry Lee. *Whole Lotta Shakin'* and *Great Balls Of Fire*. Both full of the Devil, and plenty to spare for me.

'You want Elvis? You're lookin' at him,' he declared. Best mates in our class of '62, 4B. Geoff O'Connor sang alright, played a Maton guitar. Our lead singer, Daryl 'Spook' Spencer, after Spencer Spook, a comic book ghost, and our Spook that same skinshade. Further recruits, from 4B and other classes. Graham Hudson played lead guitar for a while. As did a gifted player who went on to some of the nation's best bands across a score of summers, Phil Wooding. Our drummer, Michael Carmody, not up to much. Owned a drumkit, so the only boat in our harbour and needs must. David Kemp, bass.

Our thing, Elvis *uber alles*. Geoff and I kept scrapbooks, cuttings of the King, his coolmost world. And down the funky end of our set list, Chuck B, Little Richard, Fats Domino, and Big Joe Turner, *Shake, Rattle 'n' Roll*, with Big Joe's revelation therein, *I'm like a one eyed cat, peepin' in a seafood store*. Yeah. They let *that* loose on the dead planet of Adelaide radio. And *never noticed those lyrics.* Our band name, none recall. Lost in the white mist of time.

Rehearsals, at Geoff's and mine. Then lunchtime concerts, school assembly hall. Had to get the oke from 'Shed' Hocking. Shed's class, 5A, closest to the hall. A humourless churchgoer, Shed, so best we tread wary. We filled it three Fridays running before those jungle drums drove old Shed round the twist and he ran us off.
    Outlaws we be now. And proud as hell of it.

'Weekly dance,' he said. Densley Mills, a chunky fella, around sixteen, more front than Cox Foys, ran the show. Saturday nights, Macedonian Community Hall, Crittenden Road, Findon. The bill, our band and the one Densley managed. The big D packed 'em in. A safe bet that Densley's end of the door take was somewhat more than we saw.
Story of my life.

'Clay Trenn's the name.' The other band, fronted by Densley's cousin. He'd sung on telly, on *Woodies Teen Time* on Nine, so fancied himself as a bit of alright. His band, Clay Trenn And The Trenn Tones.
    But we went off, too, our rough and sloppy crew. Geoff, a solid handle on the vocal range from *Rockin' Robin* to *Ain't That A Shame, I Got A Woman* to *That's Alright Mama.* Spook, not so much, albeit the feral flame of Johnny O'Keefe on Chubby Checker's *The Hucklebuck,* the Big O's *Workin' For The Man,* Del Shannon's *Runaway.*

It was around now that I lifted JO'K's new single, *I'm Counting On You*, from Allans Music, only thing I ever stole in my life, to learn it for shows. The reveal on repeat playings, that The Wild One couldn't sing for a pie with peas. But, I concluded, if he's a *star* and *that bad,* our crew, well. *There's a future in this.*

'Who the fuck are these mutants?' Identical suits, cut way too flash for a squarehead job.
    They played Telecasters, knew their way around the Shadows, Duane Eddy, the twangfest of the *Peter Gunn Theme, Rebel Rouser, Raunchy,*

Ramrod. At Densley's Findon dance one night, these two rolled in on a moonbeam, sat in for a set and fair blew our stacks.

Max Pepper and Dave Williams came back a time or two. Those lairy suits, their band uniforms for the Mac Men, the band behind local country and western topliner Johnny Mac. Further along, they brought along their drummer. Tony Martino played like two trains running, sang like Elvis, carried about him that sleepy cool of Robert Mitchum.

These three, each a box of tricks full of stars. I wanted in on that.

'Well, that's all there is to it.' We made Geoff O'Connor do the dirty, to lay it on Mick Carmody when we asked Tony Martino to join. We needed a pro, and fast. You see, Densley had lined us up a tour.

'You boys in the union? You bloody better be.' This, the first thing out of his mouth, the crusty at the servo when we asked directions to the gig. At the Broken Hill Musos Club, wall to wall, rough, tough miners. Drank like hell awaited come the dawn. Which it pretty much did, down the 'Big Mine,' all the others. We went alright, said the secretary-manager at night's end. Played what they liked, so dodged a bashing. This tiny flash of glory left me craving more. All that could be had.

Our band dissolved soon after when Clay Trenn poached Phil Wooding and I. 'Clay Trenn', a nom de stage. His real handle, *Trent McDonnell*. 'Sounds like he sells fridges at Ernsmiths or Saverys,' said Densley, 'so I made him hot it up for the boards.' And a female in the lineup, Brenda, a co-vocalist, broadened their repertoire and thus their bookability.

Clay and the Trenns covered the same scapes as our band had, as well as Gene Vincent, *Be Bop A Lula*. Yeah, Gene, the Bad Elvis, skinbones jester to the King and blue ice cool. And to pull yet more heads, a set that ranged from folkie numbers like Pete Seeger's *If I Had Hammer* to our wobbly take on the Shadows' *Apache*.

The moon smiled on down.

Other shows now, at the Gov, the Governor Hindmarsh Hotel, Port Road, and the Wheatsheaf at Bowden, the beer garden out the back. Yeah. Just fourteen, me, playing in *pubs* in a *band*. For *money*.
Les jeune filles at school heard tell of it. Often.

'Here they come. The Saturday Night Specials,' the Macs called us. We saw more of Max, Tony and Dave now, the Trenn Tones on the lowly end of bills with Johnny Mac and the Mac Men headlining. But they were *pros*, playing six nights a week to our one. Johnny, older than old school, sang 'em cowboy style, those ways of Roy Rogers, Gene Autry, Tex Ritter. But between those gigs, the Macs minus Johnny played any shindig that would sling them a few bob. And, it turned out, they'd been watching me.

FIVE

'So, piano boy. Boss wants to talk.' Max jerked his head, *this way, kid*. Jumbo-strength grifter Ivan Dayman's weekly dance, Cloudland Ballroom, at the town hall opposite the Hackney Hotel, was a dry show. All the dances were. Pub gigs, confined to Saturday arv, shut at six and altogether Sundays. Between bands that night, a tap dancing duo, ventriloquist with dummy, then a professional Scotsman in kilt and sporran, strangling Andy Stewart's *Donald Where's Yer Troozers*, the shitmix floorshow bill of those times long gone and still so strange.

'Johnny likes what you play', says Max. Johnny's slapping on a face in the make-up mirror.

'What's his name, Max?'

'What's your name, Sunny Jim?'

'Peter.'

'Does he like country and western, Max?'

'You like country and western, Peter?'

'Yeah, my oath.' *Rave on. Fuckin' hillbilly shitsteam.* But this I deemed wise to keep to myself.

I'm just gone fifteen. And this, a *real* band.

Bye, Clay.

The Mac Men played Cloudland Fridays. Other nights, other stomps. The Boomerang Club at Brighton Town Hall, Princeton Club, Burnside Town Hall, KT Club at the Kings Ballroom, King William Street in the city. Dances all burbs, all Adelaide and all beyond. Steel or mining or timber or fishing towns, from your south coast crayfish ports to the far north, those vast salt lakes, all pink and grey silence, waiting for the never-never rain.

Johnny drove himself all over. Max, Dave and bass player Bill Pfeiffer, Max's car. Too young to drive then, I rode with Tony Martino. The novelty died faster than flowers in a drought. All day longs on those dull blue two-lanes, lined both sides with roadkill, abuzz with blowflies, or crows bunching at the feast. Ghost gums, redgums, blue gums, still as the dead in the heat as we fanged on by. It got to me early. Clung on like Ned Kelly's *grim death to a dead volunteer*. The dry horrors to this day at prospect of long road trip.

But the gigs had their moments. At least one brawl a night, in those mechanics institutes or footy clubs or town halls. Beered-up locals, or sometimes women, *scrag fights*. Boiled over for a few hot seconds before the biggest, meanest goombahs of the district, shy a few teeth and brains, waded in for site clearance. We played on, come what mayhem.

Like the bandsmen of the Titanic.

'Maulers, brawlers, hop in for your chop. A round or two for a pound or two! Who'll take a glove?'

For the boxing tents, for the prizefights and freaks at the bush Royal exhibition shows, spruikers out front barked out the fare within. Here, under canvas, Johnny and the Macs on bills with rope spinners, whip crackers, bush comedians called Mulga Bob or Saltbush Dan.

'Medical science is baffled and you won't believe your eyes!' Along Sideshow Alley, the Half Man Half Woman, or the Siamese Twins, a 'doctor' out front, white coat and stethoscope, declaring no doubts. Same for the Half Man Half Ape or Congo The Leopard Man, the showie medico rocking neck tatts, puffing on a White Ox roll your own. Hypnotists here too, Zumbo The Great or somesuch, alleged randoms from the crowd become chooks or dogs at their command.

'Step right up for the leg and belly show!' The Dance Of The Seven Veils sucked 'em in good, as did Venusia the Snake Dancer, entwined by a monster carpet python.

It was a forbidden pleasure planet of gypsies, tramps and thieves. No place for a kid. And no place I'd rather be.

'I got spurs that jingle jangle jingle...' And then there were the rodeos. I recall at one of these that Smoky Dawson came on to the *al fresco* stage on horseback, strumming and singing as he went, then slid off and had the horse do tricks. Bowed at the neck to the crowd, one front hoof forward, the other bent at the knee, kissed his hand and such. Yodelling cowgirls here too, or mouth organ players. Once, triple threat Rocky Page, the 'singing cowboy hypnotist.' The crowds, *the mugs* the showies called them, scarfed it up.

Between the bucking broncos and steer wrestlers, Johnny and the Macs gave all we had to these hordes come to feast on blood in the dust. The rodeo cowboys, prize money or winner's belt buckle for the lucky. The rest, rope-severed fingers, or gored, or thrown and stomped.

And the animals, most luckless of all.

'You play with Johnny, eh? I'm a singer myself.' Len and Lorna drove me round for gigs in town as a rule, but one night, I had to get a taxi home. 'I write a bit too,' says the cabbie. 'Geoff Mack's the name.' Had a song, he said, that could sell a mill if only someone would listen. So far, nothing but knockbacks. 'Wanna hear it?' Well, I'm in a moving car, nowhere to run, so...

'Well, I was humpin' my bluey on the dusty Oodnadatta road,...' A slow, stock standard country feel. In places, switching to fast bits, sounding like a blowfly turned auctioneer. Not my bag at all, so I tune out, near on the doze when I'm barked awake by his 'Whaddyareckon?' as we pull into my street. Desperation in his eyes, and now he knows where I live, so I told him it had wings for sure, to keep at it. Weirdoes like this, a constant pesky presence at gigs, a delusional cast about them, so best they be humoured.

Two years on, a sonic pandemic swept the nation. For me, all the way weird. People whistling, singing *that song*, in shops, pubs, at servos or the pictures. Lucky Starr's take on *I've Been Everywhere* soared up and stayed at Number One for over three months. Went on to be covered by all kinds of biggies, Hank Snow to Johnny Cash, 130 versions, from Ireland, Japan, New Zealand, the UK, Germany.

I took it for what it was. That cabbie Geoff Mack that night, my spirit animal, like the First Peoples have. Showing up when needed, to show what needs to be shown. In this case, for me to persevere with my calling. To follow that Dreaming.

'Cowboy chords.' Thus did Max dismiss the three that Johnny Mac knew on the guitar.

The set, the same twelve songs, every show till the death of time. Johnny's fans, like cats and dogs, favoured that same fare forever and would stand for no other. I grew to be as bored stiff as all those dead 'roos roadside. But now Max took to teaching me some other shapes, a whole other sound to them. *Jazz chords,* he called them. 'You'll need these, china,' he said, 'for when we back these other singers.'

SIX

On those nights when Johnny had no gig, or a solo turn somewhere, grifter impresario Ivan Dayman often hired the Mac Men to back the rock 'n' rollers at his chain of dances round town.

'All you've got in the tank, boys.' And these gigs, more fun than Johnny. Waymore. Bobby Bright, later of Bobby and Laurie, a rocker to hell's gates and back, bid us snap our chains. Bob could blow JO'K clean off the stage and halfway to Christmas. Had it in hearts and diamonds.

And Nev Jade, well. A voice high and mighty, *a bit like Bon Scott*, slaying 'em round Adelaide after a stint in Sydney, as seen on JO'K's *Six O'Clock Rock*, smashing *Dizzy Miss Lizzy*. Triple ultra cool.

'I played bass with the Statesmen,' said Nev, of a band from that steamy harbour bigtown. Little Pattie their singer, Chrissie Amphlett's cuzzy, Pattie soon to be a star of the Sixties. Yeah, Sydney. For now, somewhere over the rock 'n' roll rainbow.

But not forever. I promised myself.

The singers we backed really dug my Jerry Lee schtick, set free beyond Johnny's domain, banging the keys with my foot, thumb and finger sweeps, chopping solos with just index finger. *It's showtime!*

'That voice. Big as two oceans,' I heard someone say. Tiny, four foot nine in the old money, Bev Harrell pulled heads bigtime. Already famous, having been a child star on Adelaide TV. The females the Macs backed had me beguiled, every one. I'm fifteen, thirsting for skin games, of course. But could they *sing*. Bev had Dusty Springfield and Helen Shapiro voodoo. Marlene Richards, just thirteen, but could rip it up like La Vern Baker or Big Mama Thornton, full soulful. Vonny Jay and

Carole Sturtzel could sing anything. Elaine Moore from Port Adelaide, a song whisperer, like Peggy Lee. And April Byron could do it all.

April and Bev, managed by Ron Tremaine, who ran his own stable of dances and published a weekly pop magazine, *Young Modern,* in combat to the death with Ivan Dayman. Ron came to figure large in my life as the seasons and the clouds rolled by.

I was growing rich, in a teenage kind of way, and famous any way you slice it. Hoodlum Hero of Woody High, not least among the sorority. Top of that, Len and Lorna approved. I was *learning the value of a quid,* not *roaming the streets* with *louts* and *bodgies.*

Now and then, we played as just the Mac Men. Shadows instrumentals, surf anthems, *Pipeline, Wipeout, Bombora.* Here with the Macs, I saw my future. Melbourne. Sydney. *America.*

Yep. It was as clear and wondrous to me as that giant square in the night sky, those four stars of the constellation Pegasus. This music dodge, my ticket out of Palookaville, deliverance from punching the clock, for all my days.

And so I rolled on through the nights, racing the moon and stars on a soul train bound for glory.

SEVEN

'*Pink champagne, room of roses...*' Johnny Mac's one big hit, cut in Melbourne with this then unknown folk quartet, his voice, near drowned in a sea of mighty backup vox from The Seekers. *Pink Champagne,* all over the radio for a while, so we had to play it every night. Encore with it as well, all across our giant southern state, to keep it selling, thereby charting. It damn near drove me round the bend, my first giddy taste of the white line fever.

But I'd wanted to run away with the circus, and Johnny had stretched out an angel's wing, scooped me aboard his carnival train.

No Johnny Mac, no me.

'If you're not on the radio, son, you're nowhere.' So went the Word of the roadhouse prophets, other showies we encountered at the Golden Fleece or Ampol caffs when we stopped for petrol and a sandwich. 5AD, the nation's primo country music show producer then, whisked up turns like the *Doghouse Show* and the *Country Show*. The Macs, regulars on both.

And I scored other work here as an inhouse pianist. Backed singers like Reg Lindsay, Carol Sturtzel, Marlene Richards. To keep myself amused and focused, I fantasised of my tinkling notes rising past the moon and on to far galaxies. To the listening posts of extra-terrestrials.

The shows, hosted by Bob 'Two Guns' Fricker, short for Bob 'Two Guns Got A License' Fricker, his catchphrase. Balding, Brylcreemed, *a little dab'll do ya,* moustachioed. But at the mic, talking cowboy, he played the squares out in mugsville like a card sharp. That's radio. The invisible circus.

5AD also played rock'n' roll, a hungry eye on the emerging teen market. And now, even Adelaide telly woke up to it. *Say Woodies and name your drink!* was the ad pitch of Woodroofe's, soft drinks made local and proud. NSW 9 sold them a pop show for teens, who back then could buy no booze 'til their year of twenty-one. *Woodies' Teen Time* was fronted by two comperes, glam Glenys O'Brien and offsider Ian Fairweather, camp as an Army Disposals store. Both later worked with Adelaide's roughnut tonight show king, Ernie Sigley. One of them married him.

Woodies Teen Time went out live to air, Wednesdays seven PM, Saturdays five. The Mac Men did the show often with Johnny, but also as first call backup for touring stars.

'A red Zephyr Zodiac,' he said when Max asked. 'Goes like two trains. Came in cream, not so ginchy, so I had it re-sprayed.' He'd bumped O'Keefe off the top for a time there, this Lonnie Lee, a Johnny Burnette rip it upper, some Orbison croon to taste. Lonnie, all hiccups, screams and whoops as he slashed at his guitar. A beast uncaged live, they said. Blew my head apart when we backed him on *Woodies* for *Starlight Star Bright,* one of his five Number Ones.

'Flash goanna work there, fella,' he said afterwards as he chucked me a wink. 'Say your prayers, Jerry Lee.'

'*You may talk to Jesus on his royal telephone...*' Late '63 it was, a week and a whisker before JFK and Dallas when the Macs backed this fella on *Woodies.* The song, a monster hit at the time, an old folk hymn, not just to affirm his faith but to compel Australia to see that he and all of the First Nations were *no different from them.*

It took a ton of guts to be Jimmy Little back then.

EIGHT

Your bigname singers toured solo then. Used local bands, toted charts. Five shows a day, early arv to the doorstep of midnight. TV and radio spots, fore and aft of each. Only the strong.
'I've been to Wollongong, Geelong, Kurrajong, Mullumbimby,...' Yeah. I'm playing *live* with this groover from *Sydney*, doing that very song sung to me in that taxi. The Macs backed Lucky Starr at Ron Tremaine's Teensville, the Palais Royal ballroom near Adelaide Central station. A sprung dance floor, two thousand punters on the bounce on the sawdust when it was full. Lucky worked a room as if it were his superpower, and sang in an *Aussie accent,* next door to taboo then. The nation loved him for it, a TKO felling to the cultural cringe.

There were three of them, all square cuts and horseteeth. Their dad handed us our charts. *Alexander's Ragtime Band,* Lonnie Donegan's *My Old Man's A Dustman, Tom Dooley.* They'd made a splash on *Bandstand* on the telly, but to the Mac Men, the look of dorks about them.

'Their mum still dresses them, I reckon,' said Max. Compere at the Palais, Big Bob Francis, 5AD drivetimer, brought 'em on.

Well. They were fucking *sensational.* Gig over, Ron T's door guy slips their dad the earn. *Geez,* thinks I. *You got three of them. For ten quid.* They worked cheap and anywhere that would have them. Theirs was a *mission,* it was clear.

'These kid acts,' said Ron's offsider of these Bee Gees after they'd gone. 'Two bob a ton. I give 'em a year.'

'There's an old Australian stockman...' He'd taken ship for England eight years back. Out here touring this new single about a kangaroo.

In Adelaide, playing the Big One, Centennial Hall. But the Way Of The Showie then, even the stars did sly gigs on the side. *It can't last, son. Could all go tits up tomorrow.* Piano gun Wally Lund, Nine's music director, couldn't make the date, so flick-passed this job at Edwardstown Football Club to me.

Rolf's charts, *Tie Me Kangaroo Down, Click Go The Shears, Road To Gundagai.* Crowd pleasers, a family show today, his Masonite wobbleboard for *Kangaroo's* calypso rhythm.

'I do *The Good Ship Venus* to the right crowd, boys,' he winked at us backstage. 'This is not that.' Yeah, he didn't work blue that day. He did tell some quite terrible gags. One of them about a blackfella and the metho at the hardware not kept in the fridge. Crowd went berko.

Me, not so much.

NINE

My last year at school, I stacked it. Eight nights a week out on the keys, so dayside, head on the desk. Teacher's blackboard dusters bounced off my quiff in a puff of chalk dust as I snoozled on.

'Hand, up and out.' *Thwack!* Somewhere along the showbiz road, I'd lost regard for the rules of all beyond its range. Now I took to bending them. To see if they'd break. The school uniform no longer met my need to be the coolest cat in the yard. Quids from gigs and Adelaide's Italian menswear shops did the rest. My favourite, a blood-red shirt with Elvis collar tips. The *most*.

Class teacher thought otherwise. Six cuts of the strap every day I fronted in these threads. Which was every day. But I never buckled. Hell, I had a rep to tend.

'You're a drongo, boy. What are you?'

'A drongo, sir.' I sank from top of the class to the seabed. Mid-year exams, passed only English and Latin. The only choice I had looked my way and winked.

I burned out the school gates on my Malvern Star treadly that June day, humming that Hank Snow number Johnny used to do.

I'm tired of you, too bad you're blue, I'm movin' on...

TEN

'How do you *do* that?' It just blurted out of me. Musos talked high of this joint, and the piano player here, Bobby Gebert, his gonesville chords. The Cellar, a tiny basement nightclub on Twin Street in the city. All jazz here, but not your hokey trad gear. This, the zone of *cool* and *bebop* and *Latin* and *free*. Kings of that hill, the resident Bobby Gebert Trio, a holy trinity of Bob, Ron Carson's locomotive bass playing and Billy Ross, what he made a ride cymbal do.

The Cellar mostpart hosted local players, but from time to time, John Howell, the mazda who ran the joint, flew in singers from Sydney, Bobby's trio to back them. Inez Amaya from South Africa, a fixture at Sammy Lee's Latin Quarter in far Sydney, a knockout. So too, Joy Yates from New Zealand. But above all, I went back again and again for Bobby's piano. High-wire risky, new skyfuls of stars to swing on. My playing, never the same again.

My life, come to that.

'Let our love take wing some midnight, round midnight...' More jazz could be had at La Camille, a coffee hang in Kent Town on the city fringe, and at the Jazz Workshop, another hole in the ground on Grote Street cityside. A tiny scene, but *a whole new world*. They all played in each other's trios and quartets. Among them, Peter McCormack, Peter Mac to all but cops and strangers. Brilliant drummer, restless spirit. Across the decades, Mac embraced aspects of Nazism, then Judaism. Later still, the way of the Buddha. It made for robust conversations.

This other hipster, Mickey Drew, could make the drumkit *sing*. On the bass, Peters Goodrich and McCulloch swung like the moon on a string. And Ian Mason did with a sax what I thought only Bird or Trane or Prez could.

'How they hangin,' hepcat?' Roy Bates, American, a novelty in our small and faraway town back then. Talked like they did on *Dobie Gillis* and *Sgt Bilko*. Rocked a Beatle haircut before there were Beatles, and played a vibraphone, that sound of ice in a long cool glass. Roy, local rep for Xerox photocopiers, these high-tech wonderbots big as Frigidaires. Large and loud, Roy sold them as fast as they could ship 'em in.

These jazzfellas, all jungled up in this imposing colonial bluestone pad on Le Fevre Terrace in North Adelaide, or their hang of choice. I never finished high school. But here was university.

The Cellar a dry joint, but open late. Fit just forty, a tiny stage down one end. Seating, jumbo size fruit juice cans, cushions atop them. Some of them. Ceiling, low, like to reach up and touch. Some nights, eighty or north of that stuffed in there. They played records between live sets. Miles, Ella, Coltrane, Monk. Or LPs by stand-ups banned in Australia then. Lenny Bruce, *Dirty Lenny*, and Mort Sahl, smuggled in by those who *travelled* at a time when most didn't. And here, another initiation.

'Peter, join us topside, my good man.' I followed John Howell and some others. One of these cats, a name never told, known only as *Stan The Man*. Down Twin Street we rolled, to its darkest doorway.

'Here, man,' sayeth Stan. 'Get on the outside of this.' My first. Yet to have my last. Tea, pot, ganja, yarndi, dope, mull, kif. Or John's descriptor. *The herb superb*.

And to fund all this after dark fun, the good ship Mac Men. It was all a dream I'd never even had come true. Surely I'd been handed the fate of another, by cosmic mistake.

I didn't see it coming.

ELEVEN

'Has Johnny called you, Peter?'
'No, Max.'
'Righteo. Might as well hear it from me then.'
'Hear what?'
'About Johnny. He's gone.'
'Gone where?'
'Oh, we sacked him, china. This country and western, it's a drag.'
'So have we got a new singer?'
'Yeah, too right. Mark Anthony.' Good news, this. Mark, AKA Ray Dyett, a rising rock'n' roller round town, a handy set of pipes.
'Sounds a gas,' I said. 'So I guess a new repertoire and...'
'Ah, well, about that. You're a great goanna man, you know. But this is gonna be a guitar band.'
'Um...'
'Thanks for everything, Peter. I'll put in a word for you round the stomps.'

So there it went, four years as a Mac Man. That said, truth to tell, I'd grown weary of it. Ears now only for this other. *Jazz, baby.* I held it up to my ear. Heard its ocean calling.

Just one snag. No gig now, so no bread, no means to move out, and Len and Lorna not up for free riders mooching about the premises.

'You passed Intermediate. You need to think of your future, Peter.' Loving and caring, they sugared up the message. *Get a job or get out.*

Kilkenny station, busy back then. Freight trains aplenty for the factories hereabouts, and city-bound working stiffs on the red rattlers. By the time they pulled in Kside in the pale morn, packed as slave ships. Which is pretty much what they were. And my Alcatraz, the City Life Mutual Building, corner of Pirie and King William. *Life insurance.* I had to give it to 'em. Best con since they dreamed up the Devil.

From Day One, I'm stained, a collaborator in a grift that keeps on giving.
'You're dead lucky they took you on,' said Len to my misgivings.
'That's right, Peter,' said Lorna. 'It's a *steady job.*'

The supply of mugs was steady alright. My job, sorting outbound mail disallowing claims, these last rolls of the bones by a thousand chumps. My only solace now, those jazzpits by night.
'Do you give lessons, Bob?' Jazzers made good quids backing singers in cabaret, at footy clubs, dinner dances and such. And so it came to me, my jobslave escape. I'd learn a sackful of standards, form my own combo, put us out for hire. Just one bugaboo. Nothing like the chops needed. Bob G took pity and my feeble fee. Saturdays, his joint at Findon, he said.
'Um, afternoons, if you don't mind.'

You've gotta be kidding. I'm ordered to play only blues, for hours on end, with a *half-brick tied to the top of each hand.* 'Too wimpy,' Bob's call when he bid me play that first day.
'Sounds like you died half an hour ago, man.'
Well. He'd played, studied in NYC, London, so not my place to cavil. The weights, he said, to toughen me up. Backs of my hands, raw, as if pounded flat with a veal mallet. It was three months before he set me free.
'Now play without 'em.' *And it worked.* I'd learned how to *dig in*, to pull that Monk sound, that Oscar Peterson, Ellington sound. Thanks, Bob. You're a diamond.

I went for two years. Rare for the times, he was a junkie. Lessons ranged from Bob, greengrey in the face, *nah nah, not today, beat it,* to other days, *Peter! Come in, come in!* and sessions that rolled on for hours.
And Bobby Gebert, deep and wide within my spirit, rolls on forever.

TWELVE

'*Beagley!* My office. Now.' I'd been at it for ten minutes before this blobster glanced up.

My eyes crossed, cheeks puffed, tongue rolled up and poked out. I was pulling a Minda, as kids called it, after Minda Home, the town dump for Downs Syndrome kids, along with cerebral palsy and polio's luckless. These were not enlightened times.

'I'm jack of this, Mr. Grimstead.' *Yeah. That name.* 'The whole setup's a rook.'

'What the hell are you playing at?' His jowls wobbled.

'I might ask you the same question.' He blinked. *Bingo.*

'Hand in your Bundy card, and collect any pay owing to you.' He reached for the black Bakelite phone. 'I'll tell them you're on your way.'

I'd lasted nine months. I watched the whole scene, well, my freed spirit did, hovering aloft.

Fly away, Peter.

It was the only time Len lost it with me. Fair enough. Endured the Depression, the War, my olds. Score a job, you hung on to it. If you're bounced, head out and rattle every gate in town till you land another. They came on strong now, the *Men And Boys* ads from *The News* pressed on me daily. *And stop doodling round on that jolly piano.* I tried to explain. *I'm going pro.*

The yoke of the Bundy clock, impediment to this noble quest.

Now I'm as meek as they make 'em, but one day, a blue over my stubborn disposition flipped out of control. Len raised his voice, then his hand. He sailed across the room and bounced off the sofa from the fist I swung.

'Move in with us, brother.' The Jazz Mansion on Le Fevre, my lifeboat. Barely housetrained males could lease a sprawling bluestoner like this, a New York minute from the city, the rent, two doors down from fuckall. Roy Bates lived there, with Peters Goodrich and Mac, sax player Ian Mason, and Rodger Platten, another pianist. Roy took me on board his new Quartet, Peter Mac on drums, a fella name of John McGregor on bass. Speciality, the MJQ. Funky but inobtrusive, 'lest we spook the squares, baby,' said Roy.

A gig pig, slick on the hustle, Roy. We played all over. The Cellar, the Jazz Workshop, La Camille, swank eaters such as the Delphic, basement coffee lounges like Sigalis on Rundle Street under Scott's Menswear. And other places far beyond my known universe, the Royal Adelaide Golf Club for one. My next gig there, going by how it went down that day, yet to come.

At the Jazz Mansion, women too, of beatnik bongo allure, who'd read Woolf, du Beauvoir, Plath. They painted abstract, cubist dreamscapes, and the equal of Diane Arbus as photographers. They smoked multicoloured Sobranies, the haze from these intermingled with the tang of reefer in the air and spills from flagon red on the seagrass matting. Painters and poets came and went, Impressionists, Expressionists, beats. A wild medley of truth and beauty seekers.

And here, a place to practice, no imprecations to *get a job*, free to join in a jam when the mood took. A side door to heaven. And less pure kingdoms.

THIRTEEN

It was Disney comics that first hooked me. A fair hand at drawing since primary school, I'd long stashed in my mind a wish to be an artist. Off the wall weird, those tales of Uncle Scrooge sending Donald Duck and his nephews on quests for pirates' gold, jewels from the eyes of stone jungle idols. And Disney films like *Lady And The Tramp*, forced to take little rother Robert, he to endure my pick. I didn't stop drawing cartoons for a week after that.

My mind went *kablooey* at first sight of Picasso's *Guernica*, the textbook cover art for a schools program on ABC radio. And those strip 'toons in *The News*, local tyro Rupert Murdoch's vulgarian hoon to the toffs' morning broadsheet, *The Advertiser*, were another gateway drug, these rough 'n'raw tales of *Boofhead, Ginger Meggs, Andy Capp, Bluey And Curley*. These cartoonists, well, it seemed people were *paid* to have this much fun.

The SA School Of Art, oft-invoked round our Beatnikstan on Le Fevre. There, magic powers were conferred, and riches untold could be reaped from these, was the mail. Just one roaring river to cross. *Tuition fees*. No cabbage in such measure to be had as a roving minstrel. Off a tip from others who'd been there when the scratch ran dry, I fronted Monday at sunup.

'Ever swing a pick, son?'At the gates of the City Council depot I lied and I was in. Our road gang shovelled blue metal, cement-rendered kerbs, filled potholes. My soft hands all blood blisters, me, dirt all over at day's end. I collapsed on a Jazz Mansion mattress, almost didn't go back.

But to pike out now meant death to my dream. So the days on the road gang rolled on, slow as turtles on sand. My relief, the other gangers, hardcore battlers, their stories. Why they'd lost those teeth, how to hot wire a car. One Polish guy, *who'd been there,* he claimed, that the six mill gassed at Auschwitz and elsewhere, nowhere near the real tally. Wise, I figured, not to ask what *his* job had been.

Near all of them had done time. McNally Training Centre, the boys' lockup, or Yatala Labour Prison, our bluestone doppelganger for Pentridge, Long Bay, Boggo Road, came up often.

Their wrongs, I came to see, as nothing to the crimes against them.

FOURTEEN

'So first year covers commercial and fine art, or *art for art's sake* as its detractors call it.' Our teacher, Jo Caddy. 'Then you choose between them. About eighty percent of graduates get into commercial jobs.'

'And the rest?' someone queried.

'Into all kinds of trouble.'

Ten in our class. Making prints, sculpture, life drawing with nude models. The main one, Mrs Tippett, all bumps and wrinkles, great to draw. Lovely person too. Of our teachers, we paid heed with all the ears we had. Well, nine of us did.

Quiet as the stars, this one, did nothing they told us to. Yet worked, all day, on his own thing. I glanced over from time to time. *Fuck.* No wonder they left him to it. *He's seventeen and up there with the Old Masters.* His subjects, well. The eyes didn't follow you round the room. They gazed into your soul.

'What do you call that, Vytas?' I asked.

'Super-realism.' Not looking up or stopping.

'Realism? You can *see that?*'

'Can't you?'

Bob Gebert had shot through for the pirates' gold of Sydney clubland, so now I took a couple of lessons from John Crossing, a pianist at Nine. Scooped up some tasty country moves, Floyd Cramer licks I've used ever since.

For a longer tenure, Wally Lund, Nine's music director, my next mentor. How to write charts for strings, horns and such. For some real down in the mines experience, Wally set me to writing for Nine's orchestra, doing the dots to full songs, to see just ten seconds of them played, at the whim of the Wheel Of Fortune, or as walk-on stings for talking guests.

'You'll never starve with these up your sleeve.' And Wally schooled me in 'cocktail music,' jazz and Latin standards, played low-key, almost not there, a pastel sonic wash for intimate fine dining restaurants, toney night spots, lobby bars.

'You'll need this to work in telly.' And Wally sent me to his neighbour for lessons in the finer points of Mozart, Chopin, all that cosmos. Thelma Dent, a name that should have had 'Dame' parked in front of it, a face to match. Dame Thelma soon called time on me. She made it plain. I wasn't worthy.

Besides all that, I was a thieving magpie, swooping down on players wherever I found them. 'Teach me *that,*' I'd insist.

Ted Nettelbeck for one, a regular with his Trio at the Cellar and wherever good jazz was served, psychologist by day. Others, tasty piano wranglers like Tony Gilbert and Graham Schrader. I drank from every cup and still I thirsted.

And off the back of all that was born the first Peter Beagley Trio. Peter Goodrich on bass, Peter Mac, drums. 'Jazz for the fun, the rest, an earn,' I declared.

Weddings, debutante balls, cocktail parties. Foyer bars at the flash hotels, or your Euro eaters now coming into vogue. *Don't scare the straights when you're on their coin,* Bob G had counselled. *Straight* back then didn't mean non-LGBTQI, but *squares,* in extremis, *cubes,* people who lived in boxes. And liked it that way.

'Welcome to the land of oobla-dee, mesdames and monsieurs,' salutation of his every gig.

Roy Bates still had me in his Quartet but we all trawled for gigs now, no job too big or small. 'The square hook method,' Roy called it, as in fishos' nets. Band's name, any given show, whoever had bagged the job, and a numerator. Peter McCormack Trio one night, Peter Beagley Trio the next, Ian Mason Quartet two nights on. And before too long, the

Beagley Trio started to pick up jobs backing singers, local topliners and bigger from beyond the border.

'I made the first rock'n' roll record in Oz, pal. A year before O'Keefe and a whole lotta better.' He'd cut *Rock A Beatin' Boogie* and *See Ya Later Alligator* with a Melbourne dance hall band back in '56, well prior to JO'K's *You Hit The Wrong Note Billy Goat*.

At Salisbury North Football Club, or maybe it was Morphett Vale, the PB Trio hired to back this bigname, wedged between his gig last night at Centennial Hall, the Palais Royal tonight and first flight out at dawn. They worked them like dogs back then.

'How fast can you fellas play?' Frankie Davidson's hits, *Have You Ever Been To See Kings Cross, Yabba Dabba Doo, Muldoon The Glutton*, hammered out at land speed records. 'The mugs don't know whether to shit or go blind.'

Those lyrics. Wild yarns of ripoffs by Kings X lurk merchants and Sydney taxi drivers. Or Frankie's feral bushie, *Muldoon the glutton, the man who ate his mate.* Yeah, Frankie D. Our own Bobby Darin, Gene Pitney and Ray Stevens in one roaring fireball. *That* good.

'From the clubs ye did come, so to the clubs ye shall return.' Backstage at Glenelg Football Club, he waxed wistful of his days at the top of the UK and Oz charts. Now, well. 'Bounced by the Beatles.' Said it with a smile. 'Two years back, they were *my* support act. Ain't showbiz grand?'

He'd got lucky off good looks and a gimmick, he said. 'Can't hit the high notes, so I sang 'em *falsetto vibrato*.' Frank Ifield had walked with the gods. And here at world's end, they loved him still. I went to thank him after we'd played him off, but he was gone. A gig to get to, and more tomorrow. The road goes on forever.

'Well, old chum, he's not playing our town. Want to be in it?' John Howell had no trouble filling up that hired coach with all of our smalltown demi-monde.

At Festival Hall in Melbourne, the star needed help to even get to his feet. Smacked to the tits. Yet Ray Charles blew us into the wild blue. Back home, I couldn't get the notion out of my skull.

Peter. You gotta get out of this place.

FIFTEEN

'Refugee camp. Germany. Memmingen,' said Vytas to my query. Lithuanian, he said, but born stateless. In a life drawing class this day, well, he kicked off with the nude, in miniature, in a corner of the frame. The rest, something else altogether, the *idea* of the subject, its *predicament*. I began to wonder what he was doing here.

And worse, what *I* was doing here.

After class, we'd hit the Kentish Arms pub across the road, to mingle with the cooler kids from the years above us. Vytas Kapocuinas, one up from Vytas Serelis and myself. VK, big as two bears. And as unpleasant. I had the hots for another from his class, Loene Furler. But so did Little Vytas and Big Vytas. Poor Lo. Besieged.

Big V, never in it. Me, I thought I had her enchanted. A jazznik, baby, the life moonsville.

But Little V, that *something else*. As stars go, a Hot Blue, biggest in the 'verse. Down the road, they married. For some time.

Meantime, that thought with a tomahawk in its fist, chasing me round my brain. *So, then*. Art school. I tried to love you but you made me blue. And art, needing light, blinded.

No place for night people.

Gigs came and went, so fell shy of my needs. Back on the road gangs now, weary and wounded come sundown and showtime. *Enter Providence.* Mamzelles from the Art School, at a Beagley Trio gig at the Cellar, giggling about an ad they'd seen on the school's noticeboard. Paid work. No picks or shovels and plenty sitting down.

But not the skive-off it seemed. Stock still in a pose, undistracted by motion, awakens itches and aches. And posing nude as a newborn, you can't break your freeze in front of a class and scratch. Not *there*. Come summer, the flies, big as crows. Blue arsed, or green, or that metallic red. They'd land, roam around. And guess what part of Peter they liked most...

Yet on a good day, being naked and inert induced a trance-like state, akin to transcendental meditation. I'd been turned on to Lobsang Rampa, his book *The Third Eye*.

The Lob, in truth Cyril Hoskin, a plumber from Devon. But the Dalai Lama didn't dispute his claims. Gotta be worth something.

So here I be. The poses, twenty minutes each, tops. And perks. If asked to sit, I could noodle away at my acoustic guitar while being rendered in hair and skin and bone. But now and then, action poses. Just for five minutes, but hard to hold. A discus thrower, or arms out like Leonardo's Vitruvian Man. One day, my arms up, standing straight, head back, 'like you're throwing a baby in the air,' said Jo. Just then, a knock at the door, closed as per regs for life classes.

'Jo. Phone.'

'Alright, people, keep at it. Peter, I'll be right back.'

Ten minutes on, no Jo. I never knew *bones* could ache. I cast about for something to focus on, to ease the woe.

Then it happened. My consciousness, rising, floating out of my skull. *The pain, vanished. My being now an ethereal cloud.* Flying up behind students, for a squiz at what they'd made of me, then a glance back at corporeal Peter. Still in that pose. Face at rest now. Entranced.

The bubble I'd become lit out for the corridor, closed door no barrier to supernatural osmosis. Out there, nothing, but something told me it was time to get back to me.

'So sorry, Peter! Have a rest!' Jo swept in. I swooped back into flesh and pain, rushing as if to evade detection for being AWOL from myself. Ask all the questions you like. I have. Can't talk myself out of it.

Astral travel can be done.

'You know Ella Fitzgerald?'

'Who?' She's sixteen, already a star, this one, been on *Bandstand,* no less. Flown to Sydney, stayed at the Chevron.

A jazz singer,' I said. 'You'd be great at it.' Around Adelaide, she backed herself on guitar, sang the hellfire out of *If I Had A Hammer, Where Have All The Flowers Gone,* the folk boom now ablaze alongside the bossa nova wave and these planetshaking Beatles.

Our first meet, a lunchtime gig for workers at GMH at Elizabeth, Adelaide's 'satellite city', a dustplain north of town, migrants dumped here in multitudes to slave for its Holden and Ford plants. The bill, the Beagley Trio's jazzblues, and this Robyn Smith. We'd come to collaborate in time, to set the sky on fire, this redhaired dynamo rebirthed as Robyn Archer.

But back in the now, gigs thin on the ground again. The naked model job, casual, and went a lot more often than it came. So back to yakka hard. A new dodge this time, paid better than the road gang. With one catch.

'No complaints from the residents so far.' Me, asked how it was going. Too easy. At first.

'Special job today, mate.' Week two, digging graves, city cemetery, West Terrace. I followed the leading hand over to a patch of earth, a stone slab flipped over, laying next to it. 'Sacks in the shed, Peter.' He pointed at the grave. 'Two should do for this bugger...'

Dink went my pick, *grong* the shovel, slung to the dirt. I heard him bawling at me over the traffic and kept on walking

John Howell sold up the Cellar round about now. Buyer Alex Innocenti bounced the jazz for bands fired up by the British blues boom. And so the PB Trio lost our favourite gig, and working less often now in general, venues dropping cabaret acts for pop cover bands. Not the best time to flounce out on a dayjob, even one exhuming the bones of the long gone. But it was a time when gruntwork was easy to come by, in those now faded days before technology came, saw and conquered all.

So I slaved on the line for a bit at the John Shearer plant in Kilkenny, makers of those trademark green tractors. Not so bad, but tractor sales took a dive when a drought rolled across the state and they bounced a bunch of us.

I was first on the scene at the Council depot gates that day, so the prize was mine, one they told me didn't come up often. My kind of hours. Midnight start. Could go to work right after a gig if I had one on. We had six hours to do the run, three more than needed, but we were paid for all of them. Wise counsel came from Des, a lifer here on the garbo truck.

'Don't tell no cunt.'

SIXTEEN

'Well, we just lost a gig, so why not?' At a now and then footy club dinner dance we did, our wild take on the Ramsey Lewis Trio's *In Crowd* had seen the Peter Beagley Trio dropped from its floorshow bill. Jim Cane, an art school pal, heading out to this bash, in ritzy Linden Park, among those deepest and greenest of the eastern suburbs. Toff city.

I was among aliens.

Jim, invited by this girl Sue Smith. The show, for Sue's friend Trish, off overseas. And this Sue. So quiet, reserved. *Like a mouse.* Couldn't say where, but I'd seen her before. And I'd liked her then. And now.

'So, Sue. What do you do?'

'I'm a dental assistant. In fact, you've been a patient at our clinic.'

'Um....' *Oh fuck.*

'Da Costa Building. Grenfell Street.' *Oh yeah. Dickhead of the week.* But she intrigued me. Smote me in fact. Her olds, their names, *Brick,* she said, and *Noon.* Brick, a veterinarian. 'Chief Inspector of stock,' she said when I asked, 'for the Department of Agriculture.'

'Stock?'

'Sheep, cattle, pigs.'

'And Noon put this spread together?' Guests, bowling up herograms to Sue's mum. Sue, to my lamearse Qs, answers served with a smile. *She was on to me.* So I said the only thing on my mind, the only thing I could.

'I'm going to marry you one day.'

Well, it made her laugh. I knew I had to see her again.

It was about now that things fell apart. The Trio couldn't sustain itself, so that was that. The Roy Bates thing dissolved, same sad set of reasons.

Gigs vanished all over, that killing plague that from time to time sweeps all quarters where minstrels hawk their trade.

So I took to hitching for a spell. Thumbed rides to Melbourne, hung a week or so. Most every pub both sides of the Yarra, an upright in one of its bars. I'd stroll in, put the arm on for a quick earn. *Want to keep this mob here and drinking?*

And between these border hops, I sought Sue's number from Jim Cane. We bonded fast and large, a mutual passion for art. She, an ace fit for that word *petite*, hair in a bob. I took to calling her Mouse. Still do. Whole world does.

The Jazz Mansion, handy for the ways of young lovers. Both of us, turned on by our class divide, the chasm between. And other things. I, first boy she'd met who played piano and not footy. Me, spellbound by her organisational skills, resourcefulness, her cooking, hands and mind that did magic at a sewing machine. She said it first.

'Opposites attract.'

Never more so than we.

A shopfront near the art school had stood wan and vacant for eternity. Now, Mouse and I brought it back to life, cleaning, a paint job, installing fittings. Two weeks we slaved, to bring a dream to life.

'We'll show the pictures the others don't,' said Vytas. 'Can't lose.' Galleries in our town then, drabsville. Portraits and landscapes, the shit and treacle school. Few abstracts, and exhibiting off limits to any painter under thirty. So our setup would have zero competition.

The Archer St Gallery, hatched with Mouse, Vytas, others of our cabal, flagon plonk or brandy and little racehorse joints of grass for brainwaves. We hung pictures by Vytas, myself, teachers from art school like Gordon Samstag, Jo Caddy, Barbara Hanrahan. And from the local modern art star map, the likes of the visionary modernist Wladyslaw Dutkiewicz, also a playwright and stage actor. Wlad, a soldier of the Polish Resistance during the War, had helped Jews escape his Nazi-occupied homeland.

Our drawbridge, flung down to all that was *different*. Local sculptor Owen Broughton a walk-up standout with his *Mouse*, an abstract statue of my soul mate. We've still got it.

'Sixty heads on opening night. Sold nine pictures our first week,' I told them when they came calling, a journo and shooter from that top selling national periodical of those times, *Womens Weekly*. I suit and tied it for the pic. I had a goatee then, a Maynard G Krebs, but never went the full beatnik. No beret, ixnay sandals. Get you bashed by the local rockers.

'Hitchhiking round the world, giving jazz concerts,' I told journo Joan Kennett of my ambitions. 'Painting and selling at the same time.'

Yeah. Dare to daydream. All life long.

'Well, now I can hold the fort here with you,' she said. Mouse quit the dentist, left that world for ours. Vytas bowled into Archer Street now and then, but was often out turning a quid as a bush mechanic and electrician. Fixed radios, TVs, appliances, vehicles of all dimensions. His dad, a sparky, had run a sales and repair concern. Held to be a genius. Once built a TV from scratch and spare parts, for the fam to watch, Vytas told me. And a UFOlogist since forever. Like Vytas. Like me.

'You're sure?'

'Honey, I'm surer than sure.' Me, nineteen, a dreamer on the drifter spectrum. She, eighteen, practical, focused, strengths now more needed than ever. For Mouse, my star to sail by, was expecting.

SEVENTEEN

Bastille Day, July 14, declared her olds. The church, their local. Catholic.

'Don't worry, Mum', said Mouse to Noon's faint horror that I wasn't one. To be wed there, I'd require instruction in that faith. 'I'll help him.'

I'll say one thing for the Micks. They'll take anyone.

'And you will bring up children of this union as Catholics.' Padre here had me read aloud from a prayer missal. *The Confetior. The Apostles' Creed.* Then blessed me, in *Latin*. Gave me these voodoo beads, this rosary, showed me the sections. The *Mysteries,* he said. *The Joyful. The Sorrowful. The Glorious.* The three stages of a Jack Daniels bender, I almost said out loud.

'Peter,' said Mouse. 'Don't worry abou...'

'They want you to say that you'll love and *obey* me here.' I turned to the priest. 'Can we leave this bit out?'

'A bit on the traditional side,' said Mouse, a mite ashamed at this impertinent challenge to Vatican infallibility. 'But, Peter...'

'Yeah. As in mediaeval.'

'Can you give us a minute, Father?'

'*You said you'd go through with this, make everybody happy and sort out the reality later.*'

'*I don't even believe in marriage!*' I hissed back. '*It's not much to ask!*' Father Squaresville conceded my *request,* as Mouse put it to him. An envelope from Brick pressed into his soft pink palm as persuader.

Jim Cane, my best man. Mouse, none of that white matazz. Instead, a cream and pink dress, made by bestie Trish's aunt. And violets.

'In season, honey,' she beamed. 'They flower in July.' So mood indigo in her hair and the posy in her fist, elder sister Helen as matron of honour. Brick, Noon, Len, Lorna, all smiles all round. Our pals, all aboard, on the best behaviour musicians and artists can muster.

Then, a rain of frogs.

John Longden worked at the History and Drama departments at the new Flinders Uni up at Bedford Park, near the Chrysler plant. He'd been cast in a play about Luther. The role, Jesus. The whisper now, John having delusions that he was Christ returned. Rancorous goss, we decided, ours a small town full of poison pixies much given to it.

Day before the wedding, John dropped by the gallery, bought his usual armload, six pictures. No messiah complex apparent. We hadn't invited John, he neither close friend nor fam. But must have heard of it, given what came to pass.

And that same day, something else.

'Peter. Pat's my name.' A call, just after John left. 'I think you know who I am. Your birthday's January 26.'

It was her. I'd been told five years back that I was adopted. Struck mute now, all I could do was listen. 'I saw in the paper you're getting married. Just wanted to wish you all the best.'

'Um, er, well, thank you.' We talked a bit. Knew all about me, Pat, *like she'd kept an eye out all this time.* Then this.

'Oh, um, Peter. One more thing. I'd like to see you if I may.'

We agreed next week would serve.

'I have come as a witness!' At the altar before Father Barrymore Hynes, Parish of St Peter Claver, Dulwich, I hear bellowing at my back and waves of whispers. And now, John Longden, wedged between Mouse and I. *Fuck off,* I hissed. Jim Cane, Vytas, others jumped in, put the seize on. Spanish-walked him out of there as Father H flashed me a face of stone.

Reception at Brick and Noon's. Speeches, formalities, all done, Mouse and I, all our close buds, slipped away to the front garden. A discreet spliff would go unnoticed among all the smokers here.

'*Susanne! Peter!*' Mouse's Auntie Betty. '*Look!*' Going past a bedroom, she saw John Longden in there, with a bowl of water and bottles of red, swiped from the dining table. Doing the water into wine at the wedding thing. And stark naked, like he's just climbed off the Cross. I cajoled him back into clothes and on to his scooter, parked up the street. He'd scaled the side fence and slipped in through a window.

Yeah. A very Adelaide kind of night. At the gallery, a wallful of pictures waited forever in vain.

I didn't realise till some time on. Spared by shotgun wedding. In late '64, PM Menzies brought back conscription, the shit out of luck chosen from numbered balls spun round in a barrel, like TattsLotto. The prizes, tours of duty, Vietnam. Your year of nineteen, you're in their sights. Unless nineteen, married and a parent-to-be.

I dodged a million bullets.

'Peter, this is Norm.' Pat's husband, a happy drunk, shickered by noon. Me, full of angst I couldn't fathom. *Why did this make me feel this way?* Pat, a close semblance to me. We talked, of me, of Mouse. A little, of her. Then, a revelation.

'Peter. Would you like to meet your brother Paul'? She went to a room where he'd been the whole time. He looked even more like me than Pat. And get this. *He played guitar and wrote songs.* Lived in England these days, he said. About to return.

I lasted an hour, all emotion spent. I'd see more of Pat down the road. For Paul, my lost brother, mental health horrors lay in wait. Like outlaws for a train.

EIGHTEEN

Our honeymoon, well, none. Our only income, from odd gigs and dwindling gallery sales. *Got a little one on the way,* I told them at the interview, some emotional blackmail. And so did set forth, hawking Colliers encyclopaedias, door to door. We bunked up with Brick and Noon for a bit, then found a tiny place at Ward Court in North Adelaide. Of our art venture, rent in arrears now, and for days on end, not one head through the door.

I never did shift a single set of Colliers, so it soon came to pass that we were clearing out Archer Street, heavy of heart, when he happened by. 'I'll go you halves,' his offer. He meant the rent, this Henry Krips Junior, maths physicist at Adelaide Uni and fledging patron of the arts round town. His dad, also Henry, then chief conductor of the Adelaide Symphony. *Connected.* Henry Junior and fiancée Jancis Dienes now proposed a bigger space, a vacant shop on the main drag, O'Connell Street, North Adelaide, flanked by stores thriving off passing trade.

And so the Village Art Centre came to be. The name, Henry's, for an echo of NYC cool.

O'Connell St Gallery not too sexy, Peter, old man. And Henry scored us a story in the *Advertiser*. I was included in the pic they took, for some hip cred, but he did the talking, the natural salesman that I could never be.

'We're a gallery where young people can buy paintings at prices they can afford.'

And so we were. It went alright. For a time. Sort of.

NINETEEN

'He brought down the walls of Jericho with music,' my pitch for our newborn's name. That, and Josh White, the blues and gospel singer, decided it. Baby Joshua came on the same date as I had, that divisive Australia Day holiday. Menzies quit as Australia's PM for life that day. Across town, the Beaumont kids vanished from Glenelg beach. An unthinkable horror.

'So this kid's here to fix my dunny. Starts singing on the job. Fuck, Biggles. It's like Billy Eckstine fucked Wayne Newton.' Ron Tremaine called me *Biggles* on account of *Beagley*. Ron's news, local music scene player Daryl Sambell, now managing Bev Harrell and a band or two round town, had seen this kid at some bush pub just across the Vic border, supporting Bev at a gig there.

Ron called Daryl 'Sadie', for reasons that soon made themselves known. 'Anyway,' says Ron, 'Sadie plans to shine up the act, get this young tacker primed to shake the trees in Melbourne and Sydney. Apprentice plumber, he is. So I've got this flooded pisshouse, and Sadie sends over this pup. And I get this bloody brainwave.'

'Peter! Ron sent me!' Said kid came round to ours at Kent Town, to run through his set at the piano. Got pipes alright, and pezzaz by the ton. Farnham, he said his name was. The gig, 'Saturdays, Biggles,' said Ron. 'Biggest crowd in town. Just your trio. Mugs wouldn't know a good ten-piece if it marched up their arse.'

Our stage, atop a dais on the forecourt of the brand new Arndale Shopping Centre, the first of its kind in Adelaide, the novelty of one-stop shopping advertised as if the secrets of the universe would be revealed at its opening. Peters McCulloch and Mac, bass and drums, or Peter Goodrich and Mickey Drew, any two free on the day. Showtime, Saturday, ten AM, cold blue murder after a late night Friday gig. Two shows, through to midday when most of it closed. But pre-noon, the joint's full as a goog.

And this Johnny was *good*. Women, teens to sixtyplentys, the hots for him from Gig One. The mums creamed themselves. The teenies wailed and squealed, berko *for this kid they'd never heard of*. The set, a Cliff Richard number, *The Day I Met Marie*, Lennon's *Help* as a ballad, McCartney's *Yesterday*. Jackie Wilson's *Higher And Higher*, and *Try A Little Tenderness*, Otis Redding. An old music hall tune, *Underneath The Arches*, for the grans. We covered the waterfront.

The way it all got rolling was that Sadie had John fly over to Adelaide one weekend for three gigs he'd lined up. Three in *one night*, that is. St Clair Youth Centre at Woodville, after which, Ron Tremaine's Princeton Club, and then another teen dance called Halfway Out.

And between those first three tryouts that June of '67 and that November, Sadie road-tested Farnham's act each week not just at Arndale but round Adelaide's dances. Sometimes the Beagley Trio backed him at these, or at others, a local band Sadie Sambell managed, name of Down The Line. St Clair Youth Centre some weekends, along with venues of Ron's, like the Miami Club at Brighton Town Hall, the Princeton, or the Norwood Redlegs footy club. Sadie worked young John hard, four to five gigs a day across the weekends. Yet no matter where or when, young John brought 'em to the boil like no-one we'd ever seen.

Here in our town, a star was born.

But how John made it through those months, past all realm of comprehension. Sadie Sambell drove him to and from Adelaide each weekend, Sadie's white leather slip-on vamp hard on the accelerator all the way. This, at the insistence of John's parents, for dingo dawn start at John's Melbourne plumbing job weekdays.

The rumours, quick to sprout and spread. Sadie, all red velvet flares, open neck body shirts and medallions on chains, given to flouncing tantrums, and had a hand in running the underground gay dances round town. Promo for these by word of mouth only, as 'importuning for immoral purposes,' as the cops tagged it, was still illegal. Clear as raindrops, Sadie's major crush on John, but no less plain to us, it would go forever unrequited.

Sadie bought all of John's stage clothes, flared suits in mauve or primary colours, cravats, frilly shirts with puffed sleeves. Or a white skivvy under the jacket, with shoes to match. He once had John photographed shirtless, thumbs thrust into the front of his strides, and painted on his skin, *Dance at Princeton Club Sat 3rd*, to promote a gig there. John's ghost of a smile in that shot suggested that he wasn't all that comfortable with Sadie's idea of great marketing, albeit he never said a disapproving word. That pic, John's stagewear and other Sadie quasi-erotic stylings were aimed foremost at John's growing female following of course, but it was hard not to see these things as at least in part as ploys to satisfy our Mr Sambell's need for self-gratification.

Some weeks, John would come across the border over for a longer, three day run, long enough to work all the teen venues, Sergeant Peppers on Flinders Street, the 20 Plus Club on Grote, The Scene on Pirie, Big Daddy's, on top of our Arndale gig, the Princeton, the Miami Club. These extended stints were also to give John a run at local telly music and variety shows, most of it going out midweek and live to air back then. First, NWS-9's Adelaide-produced, national-networked *Country And Western Hour* with Reg Lindsay. Off that, same network, John's near-manic manager wangled turns on Ernie Sigley's *In Adelaide Tonight* and SAS 10's Saturday morning pop show, *In Time*.

It was no task for a flake. Yet John, bright as rainbow lorikeets, chirpy as hell at every gig. Ambition and stamina the sole drivers perhaps, but Sadie had that ravaged cast of the pill popper, that daily double of bennies for go, Vallies for stop and flop. We had our suspicions. Sambell insisted that John stay at his pad and even micromanaged his diet. Spiking the talent's comestibles to keep them sparky not new, yea unto Judy Garland as a child star in pre-war Hollywood.

It was around August when John told us. 'We cut a demo with Down The Line, and Mr Sambell's gonna lay it on EMI in Melbourne. Says it's got legs.' Sadie had us play it at gigs from that day forth. Penned by one of those short order songwriter teams in the US, a cheesy crowdpleaser, pure vaudeville. Novelty songs like *Sadie The Cleaning Lady* sold in the bajillions in the Sixties. Down The Line would go on to change their name to The Zoot, sack Sadie Sambell and reap great success. And EMI, when they heard John's demo of *Sadie,* well...

'Can you do up some charts, Biggles?' John, signed to a major label now, first single about to drop, Sadie decreed the talent ready for the world and all its gold. The brief for me, sheets of John's repertoire, for guitars, horns, the whole caboodle, for shows lined up for the bigger bands in the clubs and on TV in the eastern states. Way it looked, I was John's musical director, so I'd be on that bus when they went forth to conquer and triumph.

Well, Ron paid me for the charts. But John and Sadie hit the road outta town without a word to anyone.

A total buzz to work with, John Farnham. Close to the only singer I ever met who wasn't a head case. What might have been.

TWENTY

Village Art Centre was foundering, and now, our strongest seller, goneski.

'I want to master it,' he said. Vytas, entranced by the sitar on *Norwegian Wood*. The teacher he chose, same as George Harrison's, Ravi Shankar, his Kinnara School Of Music in Mumbai. I didn't ask when Vytas and Lo were coming back. They'd bought one-way tickets.

The call came the same day Village Art croaked its last. The deal, six hours practice every Monday, nailing the new hits each week. Gigs, all of the seven bar Sundays. 'And no booze or grass at shows.' Sounded like bonded servitude. Then he told me the earn.

'So how many nights you free, Peter?'
'How many you got?'

The brief, not just dances. Corporate conferences, society weddings, other grotesqueries.

For Gerry Sheridan, it was all about the dough.
'Who's the singer?'
'Me.'
'But you're the drummer.'
'Singers are all nut cases, cobber. All the more for us.'
Alright then.

And its name shall be called The Cravats, he said. Lou Kennedy sax, Laurie Thompson bass, Jim Kornat, guitar. Guitar, sax, keys, to replicate any song off the radio.

'Stray from the path, they'll drop you where you stand and then pinch your smokes and frangers right out of your strides,' said Gerry.

'Fuck that.' Flipside, the hits of '66, a cut above. *Summer In The City, When A Man Loves A Woman, Gimme Some Lovin', Day Tripper, Land Of 1,000 Dances, Paint It Black.*

I had another reason to climb aboard. Across eight years, I'd played every joint in this town fiftyplus times. The bush, likewise. Never made it pay. But in England, I'd come to conclude in recent time, a real career lay waiting for me to kiss it awake. The Cravats earn would provide, like that old eighth avatar Krishna, fares there and grubstake for first days in Swingin' London, to make flesh of crazy dreams.

So I started practicing. Scales, six, eight hours a day. I'd show 'em all. Blow into London Town, dazzle my way into my own trio, play Ronnie Scott's. Sessions too. Work my way up to first call go-to, for the Stones on down. A grand and mighty plan.

It was a weird fad of the 1960s. Allans Music were casting about for sales staff to meet the demand. A handy supplement to The Cravats, I told Mouse, to get us to England sooner. My retail phase, well. I'd demo these babies for customers with Booker T's *Green Onions*, not the *Baby Elephant Walk* recommended by the rep. Can't recall if I self-ejected or was management-assisted. Either way, a brief and failed quest. Neighbours of dissuaded Lowrey Home Organs buyers all over Adelaide owe me bigtime.

Meanwhile, The Cravats went forth, a band to suit every grey shade of Sixties Australia.

Uniform, red waistcoat, white shirt, grey strides, skinny black tie. Like the nation, timestopped in a Fifties freeze frame. Hair on males, still piled up in quiffs, buzzclipped back and sides. Brit bands, those shaggy bowl cuts, still held by many in faraway Oz to be *pansies*.

Aside from the private shows, we often played Big Daddy's. Basement joint, Gawler Place, mid-city. You could cram a thousand punters into that pit if you were keen, and Daddy's were very much so. Lucky no one ever torched the joint. Was only later that Adelaide venues took to setting themselves aflame in the grand tradition of Kingsa bloody Cross.

'You ready for *The Hucklebuck?*' Compere at all too many Cravats gigs, Big Bob Francis from 5AD. Hair like a TV newsreader rug, except his own and Big Bob got it *cut* that way. He'd insist we back him to sing *The Huck*, Chubby Checker's poor cousin to *The Twist*. Every fucking show. '*Hound Dog*. In C.' Or his other vocal turn, sentenced to slow death. Ron T, Bob's manager, made mints off the guy and even he didn't like him. And Gerry, well, he'd intro Bob as 'Here's Big Blob Francis with the Hucklefuck'.

Ron T took the blob thing further. Called his star talent 'Frangers,' as in used rubbers, to his face. Frangers, woeful schtick. *How d'you hide pot from a hippie? Put it in his work boots!* This from a lush who sculled scotch and cokes faster than five sailors on shore leave.

Yeah, some nights left me despairing for humankind. Those corporate balls the Cravats played for the car plants, GMH, Chrysler, Ford, or the electrical stores, Saverys, Godfreys, Ernsmiths. The last of the Bourbons, these company execs and their trophy choppers, gorging themselves to stupefaction in some ballroom decked out like the Palace Of Versailles. Then they'd sack a hundred clock punchers off the shop floor the next week.

'Well, it could be worse,' Gerry would say, dishing out envelopes fat and full. And such did come to pass. Like that one we did for the Liberal party.

'Give me some more of that devil's urine!' Andrew Jones MHR was emcee at this Libs fundraiser at Adelaide Town Hall this night. 'They're paying us way over the odds,' said Gerry to my qualms about the gig. 'So fuck 'em.' Youngest arsehole ever sent to Canberra, was this Jones, just twenty-two on the clock. Fascist even by Lib yardstick, all mad white noise, claims that everyone in Parly House was 'half drunk half the time.' And here he was, full as a tick and roaring for a refill.

'Stop! *Stop!*' He's at the foot of the stage, howling at us a few bars into our first number.

'What is this depraved pseudo-folk music?' Clambers up on to the stage, grabs the microphone. Waves an arm our way. 'What have we here? Communists and homosexuals!'

'Easy, old boy,' from the crowd. But he ploughed on. 'This is my new record!' A self-funded single, this, an ultra-right rantfest, *Shadow Valley And Iron Triangles*, a narration over the music of *Waltzing Matilda*. Some local jocks refused to play it. Not Frangers Francis, of course.

'When you hear the anthem,' he recited, 'lift up your head. Let your voice sing out and thank God, friend, that you are free...'

Yeah, rave on, dickhead, I hear behind me, as Gerry killed the mikes. Later we saw the Honourable Andrew being carried out.

I owe you one, AJ, for what I became that night, for all my days. A red hot, never goin' back lefty.

TWENTY-ONE

For all those gigs, I'm making scant headway in laying aside cabbage for London. Enter Leon Chead.
'So what sort of music?'
'Usual, guv'nor. Bossa, Jazz, Beatles.'
'When's this tub leave?'
'Two weeks. Got a passport, sunshine?' I said yes despite the correct answer being otherwise. Leon's ad in *The News* had me intrigued. 'Proper wicked, innit. Now, I can keep the job open, chum, but...'
'So you're the bandleader or just the agen...'
'Both. All the more for us, innit.'
'So you're the guitarist? The....?'
'Bass man, me. Born playing it, this gear.' But I'd not once heard of him.
'Who you played with round town?'
'Get serious, mate. Based in London, me. *Premier League,* sunshine. Only come back here to slap these bands together for the boats. Got the contract, son. The *Queen Mary,* the *Oriana,...*'These, the five star liners of the day. 'And the birds on these vessels, chum. Get three shandies in 'em, like, and, well. Am I painting a picture here, cock?'
We'd play the first class lounge each night, he said. Accom, three squares a day, drinks and ride for free. And paid for it.
Anchors aweigh.

'Tell him I sent you, Biggles.' I needed someone of *good character* to vouch for my passport application. Ron T, close as it got. Ron also gave me a letter of introduction to lay on Sir Robert Helpmann, famed dancer and actor out of Mt Gambier, who'd won acclaim and renown in the UK and beyond. 'Bobby' could line up anything I needed, said Ron.

I couldn't see how this *confirmed bachelor,* as they used to say, could be of use. Me fresh off the boat asking for *help* might give Bobby a whole lotta wrong idea. Still, Helpmann was connected as hell in the West End and film biz, so who knows? I stashed the letter and kept at those scales.

'Where's Leon?' Rehearsals, my joint. Leon set it up, then didn't front. Gave us a set list, but no book, no charts, just song names over the phone. *Night And Day, Corcovado, Michelle, And I Love Her, One Note Samba.* So we three put it all together. Wayne Butcher, guitar and vocals. Bobby Carter, drums. Hot players, and Wayne sang 'em sweet 'n' low like Sinatra. 'Can't go wrong,' he said.

Famous last words.

'Must be the food.'

'No, honey.' Mouse, an olive shade of grey, as poor Josh grizzled and wailed. The *SS Patris,* once a cattle freighter, refurbed as passenger liner. Our cabin, rough, prison cell basic. Josh teething. Both fell seasick soon as we made open water, for the whole voyage. Me, spared. An undeserved deliverance.

'What's that fucking noise?' Leon.He had this brand new Framus bass, like Bill Wyman's, but all these wrong notes. Just let his fingers fall where they may. We stumbled through a set covering for Fumblethumbs as best we could. The punters didn't notice overmuch, transfixed by Leon's schtick between songs. A great compere, a real wide boy sweet talker. I guess it comes natural to con men.

'What's your fucking game, pal?' We cornered him after the show.

'To get back to Blighty, chum,' he smiled. 'Don't have the fare, innit.'

'So the bread for this new bass?'

'Owner wasn't using it, like.' Sighed. 'Not at the time, anyway.'

Leon improved on the beast of four, assist from Wayne and me. I made the blagger sit with me at the piano dayside in the empty lounge, take lessons. But here we be now, six nights a week, six weeks of that, beset all about by the ocean sea. *No escape.*

Two bands on this tub. On our breaks, I hung out with the Greeks playing the other lounge. They taught me some of what I called 'Greek mountain music.' Like Appalachian hill country stuff, or bluegrass. And they had Ouzo they loved to share, much needed for the moxie to break it to Mouse. Three weeks out from dry land, Leon dropped it on us. *No pay* for this gig, only passage and accom.

He never knew how close he came to going over the side that night.

'Gorblimey teddy, lads. We're here, innit.' Well, sort of. Our ship, under a Greek flag, so didn't go all the way to England, another detail Leon kept *schtum*. Piraeus, the port of Athens, the funk and filth of its factories and container terminals, glared back at us. The bus, a twenty minute ride to that ancient fulcrum of crumbled empire.

Yeah. Athens. Cradle of democracy, Western philosophy, science, medicine, drama. But the day we rolled in, a giant slum, the grimy, threadbare vibe of Havana or Kingston, but none of their colour or joy, and a fug of moonstone pollution, noisy old bangers in swarms. Our saving grace, first sight of the Acropolis. The Parthenon. No time to climb it. Had a ferry to catch.

Fourteen hours, hard seats. The cheapest. Mouse and I, three suitcases, no wheels on them in those days. Pushing a pram. *And* a Farfisa organ and amp, plus a big bag of nappy changes. The others, luggage and instruments too. The look of us, not fortune seekers now, but refugees.

Dazed and bedraggled, we chugged into the port of Brindisi. Train to Roma, five hours, carriages so packed, we had to sprint to one not yet full, chuck our stuff in through the windows, to secure it. Italians don't do queues. Redeyed and jangled, we rocked and swayed toward the Eternal City.

'Fret not, chum. Your Uncle Leon knows a geezer.' He swore he'd line up some work when we hit London's Charing Cross Station. This, never part of the deal. Maybe a twinge of conscience. Or all part of his play. Newquay in Cornwall, three weeks, the result. 'Start next week, like. Tourist hotel, innit.' Till then, Mouse and Josh and I, ten quid in our kick, enough for just one night in a boarding house, a crudbox in Earls Court.

Next day, still stupefied that we're *here*, we're ambling up Oxford Street, marvelling and at the same time despairing at the prospect of six days homeless, when ...

'Peter! Peter Beagley!' I turned – *who the fuck do I know in London* – and this face I couldn't place beamed back at me. 'It's Richard, mate. Richard Ivey. How would you be?' Fuck me. From Woody High, one of my best mates there.

'This do you?' Glenarm Road, Hackney. Richard had copped one look at us and *knew*. But even the divine intercession of the cosmos has its flaws. Julie, his squeeze, didn't take to Mouse, plain as craters on the moon. Best not overstay. I saw blood on the walls.

Leon wangled a motor from his fam, or so he said, and drove us down. It's winter, so not high season in seaside Cornwall. Small crowds, an earn not great, but the hotel owners clucked and doted on little Josh. Christmas now 'and we're quids in,' as Leon had it, so Mouse, little Josh and myself went the full Santa. A terrific memory.

'I know this bloke,' said Leon. 'A real jack the lad.' Come New Year, more gigs, he claimed, but not in London, and that town my Promised Land, ditto Wayne and Bobby, so we gave it a miss and piled our worldlies onto that train at Newquay. Three weeks' pay from the job, but a banger Christmas and New Year's Eve, so now, between Mouse and I, again, just ten quid to call our own. Way it is. I don't do life insurance.

'Sure, Peter, no problem, long as you like.' So I called Vytas. At Richard's, Julie's about to reach for a cleaver, so he gave me V's number. They'd gone to Vytas and Lo's wedding here. V and L, jungled up in this big pad on the Portobello Road.

'You've gotta see this freak.' Vytas had found his way into the London scene, playing his sitar he'd built in India, opening for Tyrannosaurus Rex, later T Rex, and this kid from Brixton. Whiteface makeup, transgender threads, mime, said Vytas. 'One wild act.' A gig coming up at the Roundhouse, but no free door list for supports. Mouse and I too broke to go see David Bowie In The Days Before Ziggy.

Vytas and Lo, pals here to stars. He'd get talking, have them enraptured. Mates with Eric Clapton, for one, but it was more like Eric was *his* mate. Guru Vytas, The Sorcerer. And V and L had chummed up with a shy teen the music mags were calling the new Clapton. He didn't know it yet, but Mick Taylor would soon stand in the dead man's shoes of Brian Jones.

Vytas and Lo's pad, shared with a come and go cast of freaks, and a band. Their leader, Latin teacher specs and a black Les Paul. They had a flautist, *a la* Jethro Tull, and a mellotron like the one the Beatles had used on *Sgt Pepper,* a keyboard that sounded like strings, in a doomsday kind of way.

Their name, too much. *King Crimson.* A colour that can't decide if it's red or purple. And *loud.* I'd just got Josh down one afternoon when from downstairs, the sound of the end of days. He of course woke, commenced to shriek and howl.

'Fellas,' I said when I'd stood there long enough for them to notice me and stop. 'Got a bub upstairs,' just as Josh obliged me from above, a scream that could crack skulls, 'could I get you to give it a rest for a bit?'

They'd clicked I was Orstralian, so a noxious pest, but complied. Six weeks on, Mouse and I found our own place, a hovel on Glenarm Road, Clapton. It beat being homeless. Just.

TWENTY-TWO

The Pied Bull, Islington. Etta James, Louis Armstrong, Joan Baez, Sarah Vaughan, Donovan, a bevy of heavies, had all played here, their photos on the walls testament to this.
'An irie vibe, Petah,' he said. 'I be bookin' us in there soon.' Weeks I'd been poking around, a quest headed south of nowhere. In his ad in *Melody Maker*, singer Ray Morris claimed pedigree of a band riding high at the time. 'The Foundations, mon,' he said, passing a fat joint. '*Now That I've Found You, Build Me Up Buttercup*, all dem hits. That be me, righteous and true.'

Truth of it, a roadie for that outfit, Ray, but no fib that he knew Chris Welch, *Melody Maker's* marquee journo. Also a drummer was Chris, keen to play, 'come at it from the other side,' he said. Even better, Ray hooked ace bassplayer Tex Maykins, fresh from Georgie Fame's road band. Heavyweights both. And *one heartbeat from the top*.

'In the groove, Peter. I'd rate you one of just three good players around at the mo,' said Chris at our first blow. Boosted my mood no end. And my curiosity.

'Who the others?'

'Well, Nicky Hopkins, natch. And Reg Dwight.'

'Who?'

'From Bluesology. Long John Baldry's thing. A deal with the devil, Reg, I shouldn't wonder.'

Reg Dwight. No wonder he changed it to Elton John.

The Ray Morris Set included some blues, so musos could sit in. And pulled some real stars. Surely a big in on my road to Elysium. The gig, Sunday nights. Six to ten-thirty. Four sets, fifty minutes each, said Ray.

'What?' I said. 'You know how many songs that is?'

'Nah, it be cool, Petah, mon. Some bredren sit in, jam on dat t'ing, all the idren happy.'

Fair enough. I've always chased that high, flying with one of the engines on fire.

Or both.

This dollop of shit. My feeble Farfisa, toted all the way to this kingdom of fog and rain, no match for a heavy music town. Bassman Tex rode to my rescue.

'Fret not, digger. I know where be a B3 with all the trimmings.' The owner of this mighty Hammond, an occult obsessive, said Chris, more than somewhat eccentric, got about in psychedelic cloaks. His band the Organisation, with John McLaughlin, Ginger Baker, Jack Bruce, had dominated round London while they'd lasted.

But now, of Graham Bond, said Tex, 'Alas, abiding forlorn he be, in one of Her Majesty's two-stars.' Busted, nicking goods to hock for smack. His Hammy, sitting unloved in a rehearsal room somewhere across town. And Ray had 'acquired' Bondy's Transit van. 'No use to that poor bwoy where he be. But handy carriage for we in need.'

'A liberation fair and square, my liege,' said Tex.

'*Ya mon.*'

At the Pied Bull, Vytas would open with a set on sitar, then the Ray Morris Set ripped into it. No big quid. But for Mouse, Josh and Peter, about to be put off at that whistle stop called Destitution, a start.

Ray, a damn fine singer. Tex Maykins, major chops. Chris, reet petite on the drums. And for a time, we had a conga player, Mahmood, also late of Georgie Fame's Blue Flames, for some jungle steam. Ray's pals, singers and players from Jamaica or Trinidad, came and went. A glorified blow, truth of it. Loose as hell. The whole scene in London a bit like that.

A lot like that.

'Can I drop in, mate?' The look of a prophet, this one. Beard, clad in white, toting a sunburst Les Paul. Shy, timid even. *But whoa. Painted Monet with sound.*

'That was something else, man,' I said as we packed up. 'Who is he? We should get him to joi...'

'Jesus, Peter,' said Chris, through a chuckle. 'Do you not have a clue?'

'You've been playing with *Greeny*, good sir knight,' said Tex.

'Greeny,' I said. 'Yeah, he goes alright. What, does he play in a band?'

'Um, yeah.' Chris. 'You could say that.' Looked at Tex. *Is he always this dense?*

'Peter, my man,' said Tex, 'ever hear of Fleetwood Mac?'

'Yeah,' I said. They played a pub near us. I'd clocked their name on posters there, but not checked them out. 'That name,' I said. 'Bit folkie for me. All gnomes on toadstools and tankards of mead.'

'Peter,' said Chris,' It's a blues band. Ex-John Mayall, most of 'em.'

'First single just out, 'said Tex. '*Black Magic Woman.* You've not heard it?'

Well, then. *Peter Green.* But I didn't know that. Didn't listen to the radio. Not since we'd hocked it.

'He just handed me my arse on a tray,' was all I could say. He fanged out his new single, Randy Newman's *Simon Smith And His Amazing Dancing Bear* solo, then a blues on the Hammy with Ray, Tex and Chris. He'd split The Animals a while back to do his own thing, his Vox Continental the one you hear slicing through their first hits.

'My ladies and gentledom,' said Tex. 'Prithee welcome, Mr *Alan Price!*'

'How about we get Clive up, Peter?' Me, no clue who this *Clive* was. So forget it. Word from Chris was that Jeff Beck and Jeff's singer, this young head-turner called Rod Stewart, might be in tonight. So I'm mad keen for *them* to see *me*.

'Can yon Clive get up now?' Two numbers on, I ignored Tex again. Clive *who?* But he wouldn't let it go. 'Come on, Peter. For by my troth, yon Clive can make that Hammy talk.'

'Who the fuck is *Clive?*'

'That'd be me, mate. How would you be?' *Oh.* The face to this voice. *Georgie Fame.* One of England's biggest stars. *Clive* his real name, and ex-bandmate Tex called him thus. Who the fuck is Clive climbed aboard that B3 and cut me to shreds. Welcome to A Grade, Peter.

'Weh yuh ah se, Petah?' He meant *what are you saying?* Me, used to being on time for gigs, so I gave Ray a bake after this pub's booker complained. But Ray ran on Rasta time. More work beyond the Pied Bull now for the Ray Morris Set, but he'd rock up an hour late. Two hours. Or forget to tell some band members it was on.

Tex and Chris jumped ship when it got messy. Ray brought in more and more Jamaicans. Horn players, percussionists. Never the same twice. Two bassplayers for the same gig, double-booked, or two drummers, or a guitar player but no bassplayer. One night I looked up. Nine of us on a stage fit for three. No setlist now, instead, Ray's 'songs', really just reggae grooves. To Ray, this chaos all irie.

'Stick with I and I, Petah. We make war in-a Babylon.'

TWENTY-THREE

'And now I and I hit de road, Jack.' The Ray Morris Set took to touring all over England. I had no clue how a hot mess like Ray lined it all up, but gigs gushed forth now as if water from the split rock of Moses. 'Here,' he said one day. 'You de white boy in de band, you have de privilege.' Tossed me a bag big as the Beatles. 'Roll 'em up righteous now, Petah.'

They just laughed when they saw. 'Oh, chaka chaka. You run out of skins, mon?' My skills ran to four papers. Their starting point, twelve skins or better. But some on the job training and I had it beat. Long as your arm. Thick as it too.

'Dat de way, Petah. Bless up.'

Mouse and I moved to a tiny scuzzpit in Hackney, a bedsit, all our budget could serve. For me, a flop between runs Up North or the Midlands. For Mouse, a round the clock baby care centre, a fifteen month old toddler, all that entails. Little help from me beyond kicking in bread for food and shelter. Ale-drenched fivers and tenners sustained us. Up to a point.

'Petah, it is our gift to Mouse. Its provenance need not be concernin' you.' I'd asked them in for a pipe when they dropped me home after a week away, and here they be, back next day.

'But, Winston,' I said,' it's stolen.' Every second Jamaican I met was called Winston.

'Petah, you be leavin' Mouse here with no way to relieve the tedium of her duties.' The brand new TV set stared at me with the same reproval as these yardies.

'Well, bless you, boys,' said Mouse. 'You're very kind.'

'Ya mon, my good woman,' said Carlton. Every Jamaican not named Winston was called Carlton. 'Petah. You mind you treat her right.'

We worked all over. Basement clubs for rude boys, for West Indian Geordies, Brummies, Scousers, Mancs. Band members late, by hours, not minutes. Shows blown out. Or only three of us made the date, so Ray would hit up players from the other acts to dep. Or we just played three piece. But bookers wouldn't pay half a band.

'No, man. Your gig, three days ago, innit.' Betimes I'd rock up and be the only one who did. Misinformed. Or we'd all front, to find that the booking was for a week back.

These clubs, all off the grid. Had to be clued up by the Jamaicans to even know where they were, and not always welcome as the only paleface in show. *Who be lettin' in the white trash, mon?* I'd win cautious new friends with kutchies of twelve skins or greater. But their ancestry, sub-Saharan Africa, abductees of white slavers from the Spanish Main.

That meant *me*.

'There must be blood and fire in-a Babylon now!' It was that April day in '68. A basement club in London, a news flash on the TV behind the bar. Rifle shots in Memphis, Dr King, and a roomful of blazing eyes swung my way.

Mi gaan, Ray.

'Piano man's quit, the *schmutz*.' Their thing, gypsy jazz, as per Django Reinhardt, Stephane Grappelli, the Hot Club du France. Two guitar players, a fiddler, and me.

'Man,' I said, 'I can play this with my *toes.*' The tryout for Les Nuages, in Liverpool. Just enough spare change to scrape up train fare. But the gig, a season, and the best part, not in England, now become a bringdown. A family holiday, just the ticket.

Oh, Vienna. The art at the Belvedere Museum, the palaces of the mad Hapsburgs, all on my *fuckyeah* list. Too bad we're playing Kirchdorf Ski Resort, Innsbruck, five hours west of there. Oh, well.

And the show, a long haul. Six to ten PM, four sets. Hot players, Les Nuages, but didn't socialise. Dayside, they hid in their rooms from 'the Germans'. But for me, the only goy in the band, a good time was found, and a babysitter for Josh, so Mouse could join me for mulled rum drinks, knockout food. The Austrians, fab. We wanted to learn a bit of *Deutsche,* and they, mad keen to help. Could think of worse places to learn a language.

Fun stuff with little Josh too, making snowmen, snowballs. Mouse and I went on the Kitzbuheler Alpen mountain rides, some hardcore cycling with guides. And our first go at skiing. That's when I broke my leg.

West Germany as it was back then, studded with US bases, first responders to render Russia smoke and cinders should the Cold War turn Hot. I'm in plaster now, crutches to get around, the resort run done. But the show must go on.

'It's an extra gig, Peter. A sack of cash. Just GIs. Schmucks starved of music.' Bells in my head. The ones at crossings for oncoming trains.

'Did you tell them what we play?'

'Um, yeah.'

Um. A tell right there. I braced for come what may and all its monsters.

No surprise. The dogfaces didn't care for us. Told we're an R'n'B outfit, and the truth far west of that. So the vibe, a bit tense. But set to cruise control on free Jack D, I hobbled round while the rest of Les Nuages huddled in the darkest corner they could secure, and got talking with some of the brothers.

'We be shippin' out tomorrow.'

'Oh yeah. Where to?'

'Vietnam, my man. The *Nam.*' This mess hall, full of them. Most, late teens at best by the looks.

I wondered how many would still be alive three months from now.

'It was when Townshend gave Daltrey the arse for a bit.' Boz Burrell almost joined The Who back in '65. After that, sang for a band with Ian

McLagan of the Faces, nee Small Faces, called Boz People. 'Me? Coltrane. Mingus, Miles, you know,' he said when I asked. Click clack, two souls, one wavelength. Our new band, to be called Boz. 'Good and short,' he said. 'Not too hard for your average herbert.'

Boz pulled in Tex Maykins on bass, and a stringbuster from the disintegrating Walker Brothers, Colin Pincott. Drummer, Roy Mills. Mighty player, gargantuan pillhead.

After Ray Morris and Les Nuages, Boz was a whole other jug of wine. Loud, as in blisters in your ears. Colin didn't hear when I suggested some light and shade.

'That bloody amp. You must be half deaf.'

'Half *wot?*' That said, Col well up there, went places Jimi did. Hard not to, Hendrix in our midst, a living god and a pal to Vytas.

Boz, a born showie. He'd re-emerge as a bass player later on with King Crimson and Bad Company, but here, a hands-free singer. Pranced round the stage, white guy burls at James Brown moves.

'Forsooth, the hardest jerkin' man in show bidness,' said Tex. Not to his face. On occasion, the Boz quintet was augmented by a harmonica player, a traveller called Duffy Power. A face about the place, Duffy, one of those instant poodles Pommy pop stars along with Cliff Richard, Billy Fury, Georgie Fame, all that crew back at the dawn of the 60s.

So quite the collective profile, Boz. The pubs we played grew bigger, and thence to the ballrooms and those workingmen's clubs we went, all over England's green and pleasant.

But rough seas every time we took the boat out. All in Boz, bar me, registered addicts, on the gear. You could do that in England then. Shoals of musicians took advantage. So someone or other was dopesick all the time, too greened out to gig. When we did play, stops at clinics, doctors or *elsewhere* on the way, to score. Much of my earn, my guess, found its way into the clammies of pharma providores.

The first of what came to be the *Basement Tapes* surfaced about now, as part of a double bootleg, *The Great White Wonder*. People stampeded to track their takes of these new bangers as Dylan's people sent demo singles to those deemed worthy. In England, Brian Auger and Julie Driscoll hit big with *This Wheel's On Fire,* Manfred Mann, *The Mighty Quinn.*

Boz too, one of these Chosen. EMI liked his style. The white label that came our way, Bob D's demo of *I Shall Be Released,* the flip, *Down In The Flood.* EMI had free studio time at Olympic or Trident, midnight to dawn, those rockstars whose deals paid for twenty-four hour lockouts gone home to their mock-Tudor mansions in Surrey or Kent. Bar the Stones, it was said, who only kicked off at two AM. Or later.

'You've got an hour left, man.' *Released,* nailed in two takes, so I figured we'd do *Down In The Flood.*

'OK, boys,' said Boz. '*Light My Fire.*' Seems strange now, but we did this Doors hit live, so we could track it fast. And, according to Boz, this was an in for a record deal here. Standard industry practice then, releasing several versions of the one song. Royalties galore if they all scored airplay. Plain brown banker's bags found their way all by themselves to DJs to make it so.

Yet I was melancholy at the session. Mouse had decreed that very morning what must now come to pass. Arse out of our flares, couldn't make the rent, threats of eviction by thugs. Skipping meals so Josh could eat.

Brick and Noon, stoked to get their grandson back, stumped up for Qantas tickets. I knew I was shit out of choices. Here I was, at last headed somewhere other than nowhere. But they just shrugged, those Fates on high. Bounced me off that train.

TWENTY-FOUR

'Geezus, Peter. Haven't you heard?' Six o'clock closing, *finito*. Open till ten now, so Adelaide pubs doing live music after sundown. Stole from the dry venues every groover in town aged twenty-one and up, more when the legal drinking age was cut to 20 in this year of '68, and then to 18 three summers up the line. The no-grog teen shindigs, now at Stage One of the three that would follow, to that unspeakable inevitable.

And hip to the new global zeitgeist, some local bands forsaking the pop covers. The brand new bag now, heavy blues, a la Blue Cheer, Cream, Quicksilver Messenger Service, Canned Heat, Jeff Beck Group, Iron Butterfly. Round Adelaide, a host of soundalikes. The Abraham Lott Blues Band, Five Sided Circle, Bucket, Resurrection, Hard Time Killing Floor, Inside Looking Out, The Syssys.
The old order changeth.

Of the no-booze teen hangs, as well as the Princeton Club, Sergeant Pepper's, The Scene, 20 Plus Club, smaller joints had opened up, strip-lit in ultra-violet, psychedelic posters in dayglo shades on the walls, a more underground vibe to keep from going broke. Among them, Inferno, a basement in Bloor Court, off Currie Street, or the Beat Basement, another subterranean space on east end Rundle. And The Cellar on Twin Street endured still with its live fare of hardcore blues, overseer J. Alex Innocenti's companion boutique at street level upstairs, its freaky threads, hats, bags, belts.

For Mouse and I to be able to rent a place, I had to find a job pronto, to bluff landlords about our prospects. Yeah, this must be the place. Huge crates on the footpath. Full of severed feet. And heads. At

Windsor Chickens, live chooks, feet bound, upside down, were fed along an overhead conveyor belt to a gizmo which clamped their skulls. *Sizzlesnap.* Smarter birds actually lifted their heads to dodge the zapper, but then rolled on to quartering and decapitation, still alive for *that*. I lasted about as long as you would have.

'Light jazz, bossa,' he said. 'Some Top 40. What you reckon?' I'd known Doug Ashdown since the days of the Mac Men, when he'd played in Bob Bright's band the Beaumen, and jazz and folk on the side at eternal folkie hang the Catacombs in Kent Town and jazz joint La Camille next door to it.

Wes Montgomery was Doug's muse. A tasty picker, ace crooner and songwriter, Doug had three albums of his own material out on local indie Sweet Peach. Thus did the Doug Ashdown Quartet come to be. A Saturday arv going, Shandon Hotel, Seaton, at its Carousel Room. I lined up Peter Goodrich for bass and Mick Drew, drums. *Girl From Ipanema, Whole Lotta Shakin' Goin' On* and *For All We Know* in the same set, yet Doug made it sound like all the pieces fit. No surprise. He'd put in a lot of flying hours while I'd been away, among them a stretch in clubland Sydney, including that much-prized get, the Chevron's Silver Spade Room up the Cross.

'...the sweetest, gonest, wailin'est cat that ever stomped on this sweet swingin' sphere. And they call this here cat.....D' Nazzzz...' It was Doug Ashdown hipped me to Lord Buckley, hipster bebop preacher of stand-up comic Richard Buckley's creation. Doug, a huge fan, took to spouting The Buck's routines at gigs. Off this and the new wave of soul out of Detroit, Muscle Shoals and Memphis, the Quartet soon grew into a distant cry from evergreens and nods to rock'n' roll.

'Stax, Motown, Atlantic. Only way to fly,' said Doug of our makeover. And for hip appeal, bestowed now upon the Doug Ashdown Quartet, a new name, straight outta Lord B's world of wonder. *D'Naz* be this newborn baptized.

New faces as well. Up front, as well as Doug, another local singer-songwriter now, Steve Foster. Phil Cunneen, bass when Peter G couldn't make the gig. Old mate Peter Mac, drums. And from time to time, a horn section, Keith Stirling and Roger Frampton, trumpet and sax. Roger, not only a saxmaster but a thousand light years ahead of me on the piano, cast benevolent smiles upon my playing. To hose down hostiles at gigs, we hung on to some of our bossa bag, along with *Whole Lotta Shakin,'* the emergency knife in our boot for punchy drunks and despicables.

But that sweet soul music our main street now. D'Naz played Fiesta Villa at the Findon, Sergio's at the Tonsley Park Hotel, Shanny's at the Shandon. Fridays, Saturdays, two to three a night. And at new joints springing up all over now, like gold tops after the rain.

Derek Jolly was rich. Penfolds wine dynasty. Like SA's visionary premier Don Dunstan, Derek beheld a vision of Adelaide as a performing arts hub. Both helped our town to try and grow up and be something. Derek a risktaker. Drove racing cars. Imported Australia's first Moog synth and built the state of the art Slater Studios, after Alan Slater, music director at Seven, installed there to fly it.

And Derek shipped in Futuro homes from Finland, he their Australian agent. A mindblowing resemblance to UFOs, these self-assembled Futuros featured portholes for windows, all the furniture built-in, to fold up into the walls for space as needed. Derek plonked one in Slater's car park, as onsite space ex-studio for producers or for artists making magic there, and as a display model for potential buyers. Over the next few years, some of us came to live in it for a time as a short term homeless fix. Well, choose music and choose Adelaide. Asking for trouble.

'I'm very disappointed in you, Peter.' Time out for a quick choof from a job at Slater's one day. That Futuro ideal, its reverse fan aircon eradicating dope smoke in a flash. Alas, no invisible force field to repel unwanted intruders, and he comes looking, his idea of a break less elastic than mine. Not big on stoners, Johnny. I had to wear it, meek and bowed.

He'd asked me to produce his new album here at Slater's. I said *yes* and *thank you*, and meant it. The bread, never more needed.

We tracked *Johnny Mac In Cabaret* on its brand new flasharama eight track desk. The old school way, band in first, six songs in two hours, one take apiece, charts by yours truly. First sesh, Bruce Howe from Barrie MacAskill's Levi Smith Clefs for bass, Dean Birbeck drums. The other, Geoff Kluke double bass, drums Billy Ross. For both, Grahame Conlon, primo jazzer and gun country picker. Johnny's vocals we dropped in next day.

The tracks, all hits from that year of '68. *Beautiful Sunday. Country Roads,* the John Denver number. *Running Bear,* a novelty smash that year. But not all bad. Kristofferson's *Help Me Make It Through The Night,* ditto *Before The Next Teardrop Falls* and John D.Loudermilk's *Break My Mind.* The sublime, the ridiculous and stopping all stations between. But grateful eternal to Mr Mac. I mean, it was this or butchering chooks.

Johnny asked me to write one for this album, 'about our home town.' *Adelaide* spoke of yearning from afar, pining for South Oz, its fresh air and sweet wine. The subtext, the joint's good only for getting full as a vampire on Barossa Valley flagon plonk or Cleland's Liqueur Brandy. But I didn't tell Johnny that. He sang it as the hymn of praise requested, always a shrewd reader of local rooms.

Thankful Johnny asked, but I made not a cent from *Adelaide*. Robyn Archer and Trev Warner, South Australia's top country artist, both cut it later on. Same result. No wonder poets get on the bottle.

'It's over, guys.'

'Fuck you on about, Doug?'

'Flip your lobes to *this*.' One listen to The Band's *Music From Big Pink,* and D'Naz folded that same week. The plan for Doug via his manager Jimmy Stewart now, back to Sydney's clubs, crooning covers. Off the payday, Doug would track an album of new originals on Jimmy's Sweet Peach label, their inspiration *Big Pink* and the revolution now upon us.

Jimmy had me write *the flyshit,* he called it, for those vast pokie pits of Sydney, charts for their inhouse bands. 'Worthy of Vegas,' I promised. 'The big rooms.'

Some months on, I had to take it to the Musician's Union. Jimmy had concluded I wasn't worth paying. The unions declared Doug 'black'. All staff in any NSW club would walk off the job if he came on the premises. A cheque in the post saw it set right. Union forever, forever union.

Meanwhile, Roger Frampton from D'Naz, a brilliant pianist, speciality the soundscapes of Thelonious Monk, granted me some lessons. But like anyone from Adelaide any good at anything, soon poached by the dread Eastern States, for a post at the Sydney Con.

Maybe it was the scars from England. Or these fresher wounds, from trying to make a go of it in a town too small for dreamers. The choice I made now, once unthinkable.

TWENTY-FIVE

'I'll take it.' Steve Foster was working there. Told me of a job going. That grail holy of a life in music, now hot ash in the wind. Burned out and blue turned to grey, I ran away from the circus.

First thing that hit me, pushing a Victa mower round the Bot Gardens, the Zoo next door. This *funk* they give off, those mighty of the jungle and savannah, doing life in a Supermax jail far from home. An odour of the living dead, spliffs at sunrise to make it go away.

I was some time gone in that valley of the frozen. Then one day I heard the birds at first light again.

'Well, there's the Troc, the Pap, the Lido, the Bay Ganew...' Peter Mac planted the magic beans in my head, the treasure to be had from that cluster of nightlife on Hindley street, our town's bonsai Kings Cross. The Beagley Trio, rebuilt now. Here, I got my groove back, the Hammond B3 now an inhouse fixture at nightspots where once were baby grands. I craved again its feline shimmer, the sound of the heat of the night.

Our homegrown Trocadero, a shade less glam than the London or LA incarnations, opposite City Bowl. Full floorshow, the Troc. Magicians like Gene Raymond, the full Mandrake bit. Top hat, cape, silver topped cane for magic wand, waxed moustache.

Speciality, 'dove magic,' making white birds vanish and reappear. 'And you can confirm that these are real razor blades, sir?' He'd stick a pack of Gillettes in his mouth, eat them, followed by balls of cotton wool. Then pull out the blades, or so it seemed, intact, strung on a cotton thread. I didn't ask. He'd never tell. They never do.

Singers here, cabaret style, or folk acts. Young Robyn Smith, soon to be Robyn Archer, or the brother and sister Same Day Twins. Circus turns, like Christine The Contortionist. Stand-up comics the cut of Alan 'Corby' Corb doubled as comperes, working blue and dirty. Corby, our own local and live Lenny Bruce. Cool as Iceland.

'Will that be a Coffee Special, sir?' The Troc's booze license, wine only. No problem. The harder stuff came in coffee cups, with or without the java. And the liquor laws decreed meals be served, but no-one went to the Troc for the chow. Chicken in a basket, out on the tables, collected up at show's end. Then served at the second show, and tomorrow and tomorrow and tomorrow, till it turned green and gold.

'You should change your name.'

'Why?'

'I know four other singers with the same name as you. And you, the only one who's any good. Why share that with those losers?' The Beagley Trio backing her the night Robyn Smith became Robyn Archer. Keith Peterson, Robyn's manager then, a stand-up comic round town. A Sydneysider, all carny hoodoo and Sin City savvy. His idea. 'Archer', the name of the Troc's secretary.

The Troc burned itself down a few years on. Not the last to do so.

'She can rotate them. In opposite directions.' Corby surely winding me up. Then I saw the act. Pat Wordsworth, stage name Big Pretzel, fresh from Sammy Lee's Latin Quarter in Sydney. Pretz had split bigtown with drummer hubby Laurie Kennedy when the Quarter closed down after some crim shot another crim in there one night. Unwise for a witness to tarry.

Another dancer at the Troc, Alexandra The Great 48. Transed young, Alex. She and Pretz, local TV stars. Judges on talent turns like *Woodies Stars Of Tomorrow*. And did their thing on In Adelaide Tonight with Ernie Sigley. I didn't see it, but the story went that Pretz lost a nipple tassel once doing her thing on live TV.

For the B-girls to shimmy by, we three of the PBT, pumping Henry Mancini's *The Stripper*, *The Pink Panther Theme*, Bassey's *Hey Big Spender*. A whole lotta shakin'.

The Troc, glitzy but tawdry. The Paprika Club across the way, the Pap, all class, *flambe nouvelle* at diners' tables, waiters making with fire. Décor like some Kit Kat Club of the Weimar Republic. Wild. Here, we'd back Kamahl or Sydney clubland king kahuna Ricky May when he was in town. Of the locals, Julie Anthony if dead unlucky, including her take on *Advance Australia Fair*. I bear those scars to this day. More often, the Ladhams, a local sister act, or solid hometown stayers like Bev Harrell, Vonny Jay, Irene Petrie. The manager at the Pap, Hungarian. I had no clue then, but this meant, most like, that they be toiling for Sydney's Mr Big, Abe Saffron.

And if so, we too.

And then there was La Belle. Deep red décor, a rat-faced compere, it all came off here to our blues played slow. Doormen heavy as anvils, sentries to this all night skin bin. For strippers Boo Boo Bronze, Velvet Revelle, Stormy Summers, Vanessa The Undresser, the Beagley Trio broke out our best *Suzi Q, Hi Heel Sneakers, Stormy Monday*.

Boo Boo the wildest. Placed on the stage in a sack, hands rose from it first, twirling, then arms, then head, moves Cleopatra might have busted to bed Marc Antony, a belly dance as the veils came off. All of 'em.

Boo's other act, a double. With a snake.

The band had to share their tiny dressing room. So we saw things the patrons didn't. Some of the 'girls', well. Taped down the smallgoods with Elastoplast. Shaved downstairs. 'Hurts a lot less peeling it off, boys.' *Rrrriiip!*

These clubs stayed lit till four, band on deck from nine. So for me, back to back with dawn starts on the two-stroke Victa, so sleep, a stolen hour here and there. Bot Gardens ground staff were only needed six months of the twelve, but the union dictated we be onsite year round. Off season, leading hands turned blind eyes if they couldn't see you at it. Under giant fig trees, Steve Foster and I smoked mull and wrote songs. Or after an all night long, I'd rake the used frangers and Brandivino flagons out from under some bushes and drop for a disco nap.

Oh, and Mouse told me about now, a new little one on the way.

'Come and check us out.' Peter Mac's other band, all the talk. Red Angel Panic, hardcore rock 'n' roll, a few ballads, a whiff of The Band's rootsy country. But what really set them apart was their politics. Hard left, active in Vietnam War protests, played the rallies in Elder Park, songs like *Viet Rock*. Leon 'Moses' Carmen drove a Hammond, Rob Tillett, singer and guitarist, a formidable presence. Bass, Chris Bailey. Chris and I, we'd get a thing going down the line. And what a thing it would be.

So I dropped into the Cellar to scope out the Panic. Next I knew, Alex Innocenti had booked the Beagley Trio for one of the stirs he ran at Glenelg Town Hall. Twelve-band bills, the likes of Blues City Shakedown, Hard Time Killing Floor, Black Watch, Syrup Power. And Robyn Archer's new hard rock outfit, Heavy Piece. Steve Foster featured too. More, shipped in from Sydney and Melbourne. Once or twice, Doug Parkinson In Focus, Billy Thorpe And The Aztecs. It was some scene. Wild as the ocean when the moon swings close.

'Berg. It's a Finnish name. My name,' said Mauri, its owner. At a Glenelg gig, the wondrous WG Berg. A band name, not a person. Graham 'Davvo' Davidge all over it. Flautist, guitarist, keys. Mauri, a black Les Paul his favoured. Drummer, a garden gnome beard and double kick kit. 'Joff's the name. Joff Bateman. How would you be?'

A year on, I'd be thrown in with Mauri, Joff and Chris from the Panic, part of a tyro tycoon's master plan that also involved Bon Scott. I'm amazed we all survived.

'It's more use to you than me, Peter.' Vytas came home after falling sick in England. Studying photography now, he said. In London, he'd swapped one of his paintings for this fella's gold and tan vintage Fender twin reverb amp, and he's brought it round to mine. 'He liked the picture,' said Vytas. 'Offered a straight trade.'

If that amp could talk. Revealed at last, the enigma that is Eric Clapton.

'A long flight, so I dropped a trip. Flashing all the way, London to Sydney with stopovers.

Frankfurt, Athens, Beirut, Colombo. Glommed another over the Indian Ocean. Still peaking when we went through Customs in Sydney, then the flight here. Asked the cabbie the cheapest flop in town. Next to a strip club, he said. Rooms by the hour setup.'

Electric Nick we'd met Englandside, like us, crashing at Vytas and Lo's at the time. And now, Vytas had brought him round to ours at Kent Town on the Adelaide city fringe.

'I scored Nick a job at Nine as a tech,' he said.' But it's fallen through.' We could never turn away a waif. Anyway, it was meant to be. Turns out Nick had gone from that seedy hotel to the joint next door, La Belle. Here, he was bedazzled by Big Pretz, with our trio for backup. He'd perform a miracle here at ours. Cosmic forces were at work.

TWENTY-SIX

It was January, 1970. A long day. Played a stir at Glenelg, a gig at the Troc, then La Belle, now racing sunup to get hom...*BANG!* Five AM, the roundabout near ours. Mad bastard didn't give way, clobbered me, passenger side. Then herbed off into the dawn as something lurched across the tray of my Datsun ute and smashed on the road behind me. Got out. *Oh shit.* My new Hammond L100, timber case all shards and splinters. Keys, draw bars, scattered about, and foot pedals. Electrics asplay like a soldier's entrails.

'Gee, Peter.' The noise woke Electric Nick. 'Let's get it all picked up. I can fix this.'

Next day, he had Vytas drop round. They talked it over, in lingo known only to them. Vytas had heard me whinge of this beast, how unportable it was. I didn't say a word, but he built a new two-piece case for it. And Nick, fitting it back together, rewired it, via parts from an Army Disposals store, multi-way connectors. Used for military aircraft, he said. 'Let's see if we can make this baby *fly*.'

He got it purring full well, and modest with it. 'More luck than judgment.' Nick stayed three weeks. By the time he moved on, our every dead toaster or TV or radio or stereo, working again. Such are angels.

Goodbye to the Bot Gardens now. Set free, on account of a new gig come my way. A two-nights a week residency, a tasty payer and on top of the Troc and the Pap and La Belle.

'Name your price, Biggles. They've got oodles of cash.'
'What you got in mind, Ron?'

'Paint it black, son. Motown, Stax, Philly.' Waved his arm at this ballroom, dank and dark at noon, as always they be. 'Need to fill this room,' he said.

'Yeah, I think we can...'

'....and empty out every other one in town.'

Big space. Ballroom, the Redlegs, Norwood, a major league footy club. I knew what to do. Six piece, on occasion three horns on top of that, for the songs of the new brass-rock wave, Blood, Sweat And Tears, Chicago, Pacific Gas And Electric. Presentation, black tie and tux, Rat Pack chic. Between our brackets, guest vocalists, the floorshow. I called it what it was, a sonic mix to blow your top. *The Formula.*

We fast grew to be the weekend go-to for that vast mass not into the heavy blues now all the rage. Bob Frangers Francis as compere, so we had to back and endure his undead take on *Dock Of The Bay*, and Bob's unfunny gags of longhairs mistaking each other for women, waking in horror the morning after. But Frangers an easy burden, quid pro quo Ron's generous patronage.

A white-hot band I built. John Bywaters, from the just disbanded Twilights, bass. Phil Wooding from back in the Clay Trenn days, back in town after a run with Jeff St John and Copperwine, guitar. Bill Greeneklee from the Hi Marks, wayback when contemporaries to the Mac Men, alto sax. Frank Barnard, drums. Singer, Chris McClure, a big, solid unit, voice to match, shades of Chris Farlowe and Tom Jones.

We rehearsed at the Redlegs by day till our skulls cracked. For featured guest each week, local surefires Irene Petrie, Bev Harrell, Vonny Jay and Ron's new favourite, Robyn Archer.

'It's a girl!' And somewhere in the eye of all that noise, our daughter Lo came into the world on 19th March 1970.

The Formula went off from Gig One. Then Ron took to shipping in your interstate biggies. Upped the ante a whole pile more.

'Peter! How you been?' He'd gone far since our time together. Six hits on the radio. Johnny, sorry, *John* Farnham, he always detested 'Johnny,' our floorshow this week. 'And what's your name, little man?' John came by for a run through of the set. Made a big fuss of little Josh when Mouse brought him home from kindy. I reminded Josh years later, in the days of *Whispering Jack,* that they'd met. He didn't recall, wasn't impressed. Such is showbiz. All glory is fleeting.

Farnham packed out the Redlegs three nights running. Ron crammed 'em in, way over the legal hold it right there. And John, well, he worked 'em like a hot blaze. We backed all of that year's bigtime singers, their songs on the radio, keen to work our singles-buying town.

Then some from beyond the sea.

'Doesn't look a bit like him, but sounds *that* close. Mugs won't know the diff,' said Ron. None of his brother Nat's slinky cast. More your Solomon Burke, Fats Domino dimensions was Ike Cole. When he got me on the piano at home and started to sing, the sound of his voice so close it chilled me.

'Scoot over, my man. Let me show you something.' I could play Nat King Cole's book, but *not quite like Nat did.* Ike leaned over, played me the chords Nat had used. *Revelation.* 'I'll play and sing the first twenty, brother. Then you get on the 88s. One needs to work hands-free. There will be ladies there needing charming.'

I learned a life's worth from Ike.

'Nat wouldn't have it.' Ike had chosen a stage name, so the world didn't swoop and claim he was out to cash in. 'On his deathbed, made me swear I'd keep the Cole name. That his legacy not perish.'

At the Redlegs Club, with *Route 66, Mona Lisa, Unforgettable, Ramblin' Rose,* the incredible *Nature Boy,* Ike blew the punters over the hills and far away.

'We'll pull heads, have no fear. Fuckall else on out there.' Ron had booked a tour for Ike, deep north of here. Six hour drive, three-car convoy. Up front, Ron with Bev Harrell, the support for Ike. Then Ike with me. Bringing up the caboose, John Bywaters and Frank Barnard. The full Formula, deemed too pricey for this trip.

The sky above Woomera, weirdest in the world. Criss-crossed by contrails from launches, the fuel vapour turned to ice crystals up in that cold blue forever as we drove in, scoping around for signposts to the US base. There were none. But the cluster up ahead couldn't be anything else. And within this compound, a full-blown theatre. Five hundred seats, red velvet stage curtains, footlights, spotlights. And a Steinway concert grand, here at the end of the earth.

In the tiny town, a supermarket, movie theatre, a bar. Squash courts, a gym, swimming pool. A *bowling alley*, for fuck's sake. 'Yeah, the Yanks dropped it all in from scratch,' said Ron. Six thousand US army personnel here meant jobs for every local, all one thousand of them. To them, Uncle Sam the duck's nuts.

'Ninety minute show, mam'selle et monsieurs,' said Ron. 'Beagley Trio thirty, Trio with Bev thirty, then Ike. Something for every bastard.'

We're playing to US doughboys, local civilians, British scientists. We met and mingled between our two shows nightly. I asked about the nuke tests they used to do west of here, at Maralinga.

'We've all heard stories,' said one of the locals. 'After a blast, blackfellas went roo hunting. Cut 'em open, they're all yellow inside. Couldn't eat them.' For the bomb tests, they said, the Brits put up signs in the desert. '*Aborigines Beware. Atom Bomb Explosions.* Too bad they couldn't read English.'

'So what happened?'

'Hundreds of 'em. Massive irradiation.' PM Menzies had invited the Brits here, far from Russian eyes, in the times before spysats. And no intel to be had from the dead.

No nukes now but they still tested missiles. Buildings here had bomb shelters. 'In case one of them falls out of the sky,' they said. 'But no one bolts for the shelters. I mean, what would be the point?' Mimed a huge blast with his hands, *KABOOM*.

They laughed. I didn't.

'See them? Sure.' But most of them not UFOs, they contended. Launches daily, as well as research involving strange airborne objects. And bits falling off when things went haywire. 'But now and then, well. You tell me.' The place had a deadset Roswell vibe about it. I recall what Ron said before we left.

'Oh, Biggles,' he said. 'Three things you can't take up there.'
'What's that, Ron?'
'A transmitting radio.'
'Don't own one.'
'Or binoculars.'
'Never in my life...'
'Or a *camera*.'

'Well, they'll get the bent crowd in, all the heads,' I said. Back at the Redlegs, Ron's chasing the hard rock crowd. My tip, Red Angel Panic. Heavy rep, big following.

'Fuck me drunk, Biggles. You didn't tell me they were Commos!' They came, they played, they cleared the room. Footy club crowd not up for striking blows for the Revolution. And the Panic's own fans, allergic to footy clubs, gave it a miss. I had to hook them off, get The Formula back on, before Ron chomped off their heads. And mine.

'I wrote a hunnerd fiddy million dollar hits, man. Well, designed and intended as such.' One of them, *Great Balls Of Fire*, the Jerry Lee smash. 'They dug the title, but not the all of it. So they rewrote the rest. Unto me, half the royalties, you dig. The *good* half.'

He'd split the US for Europe, like so many musos of colour. 'Stranger in my own hometown, man. But in London, England, a king I be.' Jack Hammer, big in the Mod and soul scene there. 'Sho' nuff. I can make whitey *dance*.'

Three weeks at the Redlegs we did, crowds gagaroonie for Jack. Not just because he was ace. At that time down under, this fad for African Americans, deemed all of a sudden coolsville. Kicked off by Marcia Hines and others, shipped in to Sydney for *Hair* in '69. Fetched up on TV ads, variety shows, all over the live scene. Lovelace Watkins, Delilah, Freddie Paris, scads more.

And Ron T sold those Yanks at Woomera a Jack Hammer tour. Eerie place. Left me uneasy all over again. There was no third trip to the treeless forever of the north. Fine by me.

'You should see what's down there, Biggles.' This, a pub Ron was now running, the Old Lion in North Adelaide, our town's Carlton or Paddo. Three restaurants, four bars, huge disco. Beneath all that, brick tunnels, once wine cellars or cold storage space.

Ron, being Ron, turned them into two bars, a grand piano wedged into one of them. I played this baby as a solo, Wednesday and Thursday nights, Robyn Archer down the other end doing her thing. We packed in all the heads this catacombs could hold.

Alex Innocenti, the *yin* to Ron T's *yang*. The Cellar, still a dry show. Alex also ran the 20 Plus Club, before it chose to explode into flames one moonless night. And now Alex took his 'Happenings' at Glenelg Town Hall to the Octagon Theatre out at Elizabeth, the Railways Institute Hall in the city, to the Adelaide Uni refectory. Dropped in more interstaters, Wendy Saddington, Spectrum, Daddy Cool.

And on top of that, Alex ran daytime beachfront shows, six-band bills, in co-pro with 5AD and KA. The Beagley Trio, Combo or Quartet, a guernsey somewhere in all that.

It was magic to be so busy at that thing I so prized, but rare I'm home now, rising at noon-thirty and gone at sunset. Mouse and the kids, almost a universe parallel. A state of affairs I'd come to regret.

TWENTY-SEVEN

'Fuck, Vince. What are you doing?'

'Want some?' He was the first head I saw fire up a scoob in public. Fearless, this fella. Possession bust meant jail time back then. *Fuck it*. I took a deep toke. 'Yeah, Bon sang lead on *Juliette* and that was the end of me,' said this Vince Lovegrove of his band's last single. At Adelaide Uni refectory, the Beagley Trio had just ripped through a set, Red Angel Panic up now, doing the wild thing. 'But thanks to the Valentines I'm a face, so I jumped on the phone.'

Vince, one of two singers in The Vallies, from Perth. The other, Bon Scott, but clear as windows who was the better. These two, busted for grass in Melbourne. Industry wouldn't cop The Valentines after that, so over and outskie. Vince rolled across to Adelaide, hustled himself a music column for the *News,* and one for Melbourne-based *Go-Set* magazine, as their South Oz news desk.

'And then Channel Nine,' he said. 'An easy sell. Take a dead timeslot, raise it back to life.'

Vince was co-compere of *Move* on NWS-9, rival to SAS-10's *In Time* but a hip edge. Top of that, set up an agency with his wife Helen Corkhill. Called it Jovan. Great contacts via his Vallies days. The Jovan plan, to truck in burgeoning second tier acts from Sydney and Melbourne, locals as supports. 1970. Year Of the Dog. Our town began to bark and howl.

Time to get in on it.

'Hamish who?'

'Hamish Henry,' he said. At the Redlegs, Vince checking out the Formula. I hustled him out to the car park lest he spark up a doob in the ballroom and have Ron T snap our necks. 'The City State Motors guy,' said Vince. 'In real estate as well. Getting into rock 'n' roll. Sees a quid in it.'

Vince rented an office for Jovan on Le Fevre Terrace. Landlord, turns out, in the adjoining suites, was Hamish. And this Mr Henry had plans. To buy up venues, bankroll bands to play them, then record them here in our dry, dusty burg, that he might sell it to all the world. 'Make this a music town, like Nashville or Austin or LA,' said Vince.

And Hamish had just lined up Vince his first mission to that end. 'Me and Trevor, his business partner. Flying us up to Sydney.' Bon Scott there now, out front of his new band, Fraternity. 'I plan to bring the Frats down here for a tour,' said Vince. 'But Hamish wants me to drop a whole other deal on them.'

Hamish wanted to bring them here all right. For keeps, to groom them for stardom nationwide, 'then England, then the planet.'

Frats, not keen when Vince pitched it to them. Then Hamish said he'd finance a trip over to Adelaide for them to play a run at a club he'd taken over, Headquarters, to talk in person. Two of them, Bruce Howe and John Freeman, Adelaide boys, so that helped seal it. And Bon, 'up for any ticket to madness,' said Vince.

The Frats not the only outfit Hamish rehoused in South Oz. The other, Sydney-based Lotus, a young Ian Rilen on bass, that same who went on to Band Of Light, Blackfeather, Rose Tattoo, X, all the rest. Hamish gave Lotus a place to crash, on the property he'd acquired up in the Hills to stage a three day festi, around a tiny township called Myponga.

'Bon's the name,' he said, hand out. 'Listen, I need to fix my head before we play. Would you happen to...' I took Bon and Vince out to the lane behind Headquarters. The DS always about, on the trawl to bust smokers, belt some intel out of them, then hit on dealers for a sling of the action. 'This Hamish,' said Bon. 'He dinky di or just a big noter?' Besides hustling houses and cars, Hamish ran a gallery. So, a patron of the arts, I told Bon.

'Cool McCool in my book,' I said.

'Not a whack, then,' said Bon. 'Hey, where's Aldgate?'

'The Hills. Thirty minutes drive from here.'

'Cool. He's scored us a place up there.' Passed the joint my way. 'Never lived on a farm before.'

Frats knocked us flat that night. This Bon, a ball of cosmic fire.

Yeah, Hamish was going big. Myponga Festival, second ever down under after the Ourimbah 'Pilgrimage For Pop' in NSW a year prior. All local acts. They told the media that John and Yoko were coming. A ruse, to pull heads. But Myponga, well,...

'Black Sabbath and Cat Stevens,' said Vince. Myponga, their only show in Australia. To the swarms thereby lured, a showcase for Fraternity and Lotus. And for the newborn War Machine, formerly local bluesrockers WG Berg. Hamish had come calling with treasure to trade. On one condition.

'Yes, well. War Machine,' said Mauri their guitarist. 'His idea of a cool new name.' But along with that, a van, straight off the City State showroom floor. 'No more stuffing gear into dying cars.' And new backline, amps, keyboards, drums. From there, to Innocenti's for stage threads. Their music, overhauled as well. Hamish bade them switch from heavy blues to the stylings of Jethro Tull, the latest thing from England.

'Twenty-four hours on a plane sounded freaky – so we came!' This, the word from Ozzy Osbourne to Vince in his column *Feed Your Head* in *Go-Set*. Too bad about Cat Stevens. At Heathrow, the Cat decided, that ride not so trippy. And a better offer to play in LA that same weekend, so...

But no biggie. Hamish and offsider Alex Innocenti also trucked in anyone who was anyone Ozwide. Daddy Cool, Thorpie, Copperwine with Jeff St John and Wendy Saddington, Company Caine, Spectrum, Chain, Healing Force, Sirius, a Hungarian jazz-rock setup featuring a young Jackie Orszaczky, Doug Parkinson's new outfit Fanny Adams, a 'supergroup', Johnny Dick and Teddy Toi from the Aztecs, Vince Melouney, ex-Bee Gees. It was some trip. Mouse, Josh, little Lo and I joined fifteen thousand heads that last weekend of January '71. George Harrison's *My Sweet Lord* on the radio, John and Yoko's *Power To The People.* Charlie Manson and disciples convicted for murder round about now, and the Vietnam War blazing on like an oil rig afire.

Herb superb the go for the freaks of the tent city on the hills sloping down to the stage. Elsewhere, bikers, grogans, rockers, necking warm Southwark and West End in the sun. The land itself shook at the volume of Sabbath, of Thorpie and the Aztecs. And Daddy Cool floored us all. 'Like R Crumb comics come to life,' I said to Mouse. Jeff St John and Wendy Saddington's turn belted me damn near to the moon. I'd come to work with both, sooner than I imagined.

My buds from War Machine, well. All bands have days like this. The whole thing goes to smash. A weirdsville bill didn't help. The hapless Machine, sandwiched between the mighteous sock-it-to-me folk blues of Margaret Roadknight, and dynamite 'n' gelignite African American vocal duo Blackfire, never had a ghost. Then Frats, Bon on the razzle, brought it all back home, the wondrous Mike Rudd and Spectrum after that. By morning, War Machine was no more.

'Peter? It's Hamish. Can you come into Grape?' What was this in aid of? I had preoccupations. The Redlegs had called time on The Formula, switched to DJs. They're not hiring at the City Council, not even at Windsor Chickens. And my stash, down to snap crackle pop.

Chris Bailey from the Panic was here at the Grape Organisation office, and Mauri Berg from War Machine. Chris, Mauri and War Machine drummer Joff had been talking this over for a while, they said, and had pitched it to Hamish here. Those three and me, forces joined. Prospective name, *Headband*. I'd choked down a spliff of seeds and green dust on the way over. My face betrayed my confusion. What were they on abou...? 'War Machine's over and out,' said Hamish, 'and Lotus have packed it in. So, new strategy. Frats and Headband the package. Bang it into shape here, then Melbourne, Sydney, UK.' Chris whistled low and soft. *How's that grab ya?*

Me, not Headband's first choice, it seemed. They'd lined up a local Hammond heavy Ken Skinner, with whom they'd worked in the Panic and on a tour with national stars of the day Russell Morris and Issy Dye. But then Joff and Chris had recalled seeing the Trio do our thing and declared those jazztones a bag of sonic spices they must have. 'Nine, ten gigs a week,' said Hamish. 'Oh, and Peter. How are you off for a day gig?'

'Five days a week I run the shop for Hamish, and six nights playing once we start. Separate salary for each,' my news for Mouse. Hamish, closing his gallery on Le Fevre Terrace, moving it to the old stables out back of his place on nearby Molesworth Street. The opening, two months hence. My first task, convert horse garage to artspace. Meantime, we set to creating Headband, unfunded but for the dole. Our *arts grant,* we called it.

'Leave your gear here, Peter,' says Chris. Headband's first blow, a hot Feb arvo, the Hills ablaze. Bushfires near took out four townships. As per local custom, kicked off by a firebug. We're crammed into an outbuilding up the back of City State Motors. Gift of Hamish, a Headband lock-up in the guts of the city. 'You right for tomorrow?' says Chris. I passed back the hash pipe and a query, of how often they planned to rehearse. 'Monday to Friday, Pedro,' said Mauri. 'Ten to six.'

They weren't joking. The Headband Plan, five repertoires, four of them covers, to be armed heavy for any gig going. Weddings, parties, everything, to make this baby *pay*. And so it went. We learned up hillsides of songs from planets blues and jazz, rock to baroque to Beatles, and what they called 60/40 back then, sixty percent vapid pop, the remainder for senior punters dancing slow. Foxtrots, waltzes, *The Pride Of Erin,* all that shuffle.

Chris brought in Paul Hille, the Panic's roadie, to be ours. That outfit on the slab for now, Chris with us, and Peter Mac having fled both Panic and the Beagley Trio to join the Ram Jam Big Band in Melbourne. But an after-midnight gig still going for the PB Trio at La Belle, and another weekly thing I'd only just teed up at the Broadway Hotel, Glenelg. So welcome aboard, Chris and Joff.

In the scant hours free, we shaped the gallery into being. Mauri a chippy, so our Mr Henry slung him pieces of eight to do the needful here with hammer, saw and spirit level.

Yep, Hamish made sure we toiled for his gold. And Mauri and I, not the only ones.

'Bon comes in to mow the grass, rake the leaves, prune the trees, keep the grounds tidy.' Hamish turned to Bon, the reproach in his tone failing to fade that wicked grin. 'And for a sly swim in my pool or a feed from the fridge.'

Bon, broke, and Frats, for all the noise Vince was making about them, not working that much. The Odyssey festi at Wallacia up in New South a week before Myponga and now, odd gigs at the 'People's Pier,' the Largs Pier Hotel, or Friday lunchtimes at Adelaide Uni's Union Hall. 'We rehearse ten times more than we play,' Bon's take on it. 'Doing it arse about, I reckon.' So Hamish laid this job on him, to keep him busy. Perhaps to stop him from bolting.

Bon in our midst just weeks now, but a taste for hash, mull, gold tops, LSD, Johnnie Red and Harvey Wallbangers the talk of the scene. Me, growing my own at that time, to get through dacca droughts. 'You look like a head who knows what he's doing,' said Bon. 'Can't wait to road test it.' Before the year was out, the town entire was calling him Ronnie Roadtest.

'Too much, far out,' he chuckled as he hit on the last of the roach. 'Only one thing beats that.' Me, spinning out. *Stop the room, I want to get off.* Bon fished in his cut-off denim shorts, his full wardrobe that day. Gulped a pill. 'Orange Barrel,' he said. Far stronger than the blotter acid getting around then, Clear Light, Yellow Dots and such. 'Want one?' A lordly patron might lob at the gallery any time, or someone with Lady parked in front of their name, *wanting to talk.* I couldn't be flashing, peaking, lockjawed. 'Fair enough,' he said. And glommed that one too.

'Whaddya reckon, Peter?' Bon came in toting an exercise book one day. Not bad, the lyrics within. 'Frats won't bite. Too simple, not spacey enough, they reckon,' he said. 'They say work on them some more. But, you know, I can't do that,' he said, laughing. 'Cause they're finished.' And they were. A few years on, the biggest hits AC/DC ever had.

Vytas too was part of the Hamish Plan. Poster art for Grape gigs, album covers, ads, flyers, stage backdrops, band names on kick drum skins. And Grape's official photographer. Pics for media as well as PR blurbs. Bon, his favourite subject. And of course, Vytas pictures a star pull at the gallery. Bon first met Vytas there. They clicked from the off. Some days, you'd swear they were brothers. Both migrant kids, I guess, and each held the other to be a genius.

'Your brief, Peter, is to sell all the pictures you can.' For Hamish, the gallery a retail outlet, not an indulgence. Fortunate that I knew David Dridan. A renowned landscaper and teacher, David had managed the setup in its past life, and amassed a mighty mailing list of keen collectors. We opened a new show every three months. Our top sellers, Vytas pictures, or his alongside others.

And Hamish assigned me other tasks. Lest my hands fall idle, mine was the phonework for Frats, Headband, other Grape acts. So I booked gigs, herded band members, road crews, all that noise, from the desk at the gallery. Frats and Headband converged most weeks for a face to face with Hamish, to boil up schemes to put us on the world's radar. Vince and Vytas made the scene for these too. Hamish hosted in his onsite mansion, our privilege there to rip into his bar. Some days, diamonds. Others, well...

Vytas had other reasons to hang out at the gallery. Lovers, stashed all over town. His home was with Lo Furler, up in the Hills at Carey Gully. Just as Hamish housed Frats on a farm at Aldgate, Vytas built a shed on land in the Gully that Hamish owned or rented, I was never sure which. The marriage, over now. Lo knew him too well.

The Valley Of Vytas, studded with works in progress. Ex-Army APCs, dead cars, trucks, bikes, a boneyard battalion to tinker back to life. These days they'd call Vytas a hoarder, but the way I see it, a recycling pioneer. That said, the place a bit Mad Max, a feral junkyard. Some of these wrecks were resurrected, others left as was. Decreed to be art statements.

'Here, let me show you something.' I'd often bring my acoustic guitar to work, a Spanish style job that Vytas had made for me. After knock off, we'd noodle around with Bon's lyrics. He knew just three cowboy chords, so I taught him a few more. Barre chords brought delight and revelation. 'And,' I said, 'don't play just downstrokes. Sounds like the Singing Nun. Try some upstrokes.' He did. For that feel. The one on *Long Way To The Top* and *Jailbreak*.

'The Liberals? Peter, I can't hate 'em enough.' In power since our fourth birthdays, 1949, we worked out. Now, Gough Whitlam, the Labor leader, on the rise as an election loomed. 'Can't wait to see the arse end of 'em,' said Bon. 'Hey, can you show me those minor chords again?'

I think some days Hamish saw himself as the new Kym Bonython around town. This local arts impresario loved Diz Gillespie, Louis Armstrong, Ellington and Basie so much, he brought them out to tour. From old money, Kym, a wartime pilot, then racing car driver, jazz drummer.

'How's trade?' Kym's gallery, just down the road. On slow days at ours, I'd stroll down for a chat. His art and music ventures, bankrolled by his 'circus for the masses,' his phrase for Rowley Park Speedway. 'None of it possible,' he said, 'if not for the pie eaters,' his tag for the hot rod fans. Bon thought that was a kack when I told him. 'Sounds a bit like our game, Peter. Ain't no demolition derby, ain't no Mona Lisa.'

TWENTY-EIGHT

It was April of '71. I hit up Bob Lott, the only game in town. Pubs, clubs, discos, dances, the whole nine planets, *entre* only via Bob's Central Booking Agency. He knew us all well, so gigs came soon for Headband, lots of them. But our first, well…

'Some business associates of mine,' said Hamish, who volunteered Headband for this mission. 'To road test your show.' Three hundred guests, a Greek white wedding. Our set, Tom Jones, the Mediterranean end of the Elvis canon, Nana Mouskouri's *Never On Sunday* all went without saying. *Girl From Ipanema* and Dave Brubeck's *Take Five*, a lick of bossa and jazz the whole world knew. From Lambert, Hendricks and Ross, *Gimme That Wine*. Chris Bailey's mean Sinatra take on Ellington's *Satin Doll*. And some can't go wrong Beatles. 'Early hits, gentlemen,' said Chris. 'No post-acid crowd confusers.'

'Right! Nobody fucking moves!' We'd strolled away while the speeches were on, pre-gig smoko worn off, time for a re-up. Now, through fog of Araby, two carloads of the bastards. I flicked the roach over the fence before they clocked we four longhairs.

'You dagoes got a license?' A real way with words, these cops. The hosts, selling booze here, minus a permit. *Someone's dobbed them in.* Neighbours, my guess. The ones on every street, eight o'clock bedtime and a down on all the world. We lugged out amid the wail and shout, careful not to slip on champagne tears.

It wasn't Headband's last wedding. Another Hamish pal, and this time, a white marquee that might engulf Carnegie Hall, on the grounds of a swish bluestone pile deep inside the Land Of The Silvertails. Chris, myself, Joff all had bow ties to go with our tuxes of a kabillion such gigs past. But Mauri, our rockpig outlander, no such to hand. Chris had to lend him a blue silk one and show him how to tie it. Payoff, all the Dom and Moet et Chandon we could guzzle. And Anglo squattocracy, these toffs, so no fear of cops on the pond. *Smoke 'em if you got 'em.*

Meantime, a pile of 'real' gigs rolled in. The Scene disco, Inferno, Fiesta Villa at the Findon Hotel, the Largs Pier. Others. Bob and partners Ray Goldie, Joyce Washington and Eddy Young bade us be busy. And now our patron saw hills of gold in that hustle too. Solution, pure Hamish. Set up his own venues. The first, 'Headquarters,' on the site of the burned-out 20 Plus Club. Trevor Brine, a partner in Grape, bought the still-glowing ruin for next to nix, rebirthed it as a disco. Then Hamish bought it off *him* to book bands into. Among these, Frats and Headband, as often as the market would bear.

By mid '71, there were four of them. Headquarters Central, Grote Street, now joined by Headquarters North, Hamish hiring out the Octagon Theatre out at Elizabeth once a week. HQ West, same deal, at St. Clair Youth Centre, Woodville. The fourth, a pre-existing city teen hang, memory imperfect says Snoopy Hollow on Flinders or The Scene on Pirie. And it didn't end there.

'You'll be working with all these outfits,' said Hamish. 'Here, Sydney, Melbourne, the Goldie.' Glenn Wheatley from the Masters Apprentices had bounced their manager, that same Sadie Sambell who handled Farnham and Bev Harrell. The Masters being well and truly rooked, it seems, among others, so Glenn created Drum Management. Heavy names on his talent list. Jeff St John, Company Caine, Tamam Shud. Hamish bought into Drum, and so did open up Headband's rock 'n' roll Silk Road.

We started to feel like we were part of a mighteous empire. But pimping music doesn't work like real estate and cars. As we came to see.

TWENTY-NINE

'Tooley's the name. You cunts are tops.' From the Largs Pier was Tooley, one of the bookers there. He'd help out with Headband's lug, one arm hoisting PA bins on to his shoulder that took two of us to budge.

Headband's first tour now, to the Snowy, to wit Mt Hotham and Falls Creek. Tooley and his pals from The Pier had set it up, among them pub manager Ron Alphabet, called so down to his long and unsayable Polish surname, a blizzard of consonants, another fella known only as 'Black Charlie,' and assorted others. They climbed aboard the bus they'd hired with grog enough to drop a Viking horde, a bucket dropped in the aisle to serve as chunder vat. And to piss in, when the plastic bag they'd brought along came near to bursting. Such be the times.

Jim Keays from the Masters was here as compere for the shows. Between tokes on the foot-long joints he shared round, stories of where they were at now. Years of hits, *5.10 Man, Think About Tomorrow Today, Turn Up Your Radio,* sellout shows across the nation. All over the telly as well, and fresh from a UK swing. Top of the charts even now with *Because I Love You*. Yet the Masters were 'beggared,' said Jim, swiping milk money off porches, or wolfing food off supermarket shelves in the aisles. I remembered London. 'Been there,' I said.

'Yeah, Christ almighty, England,' said Jim. 'We couldn't do gigs. No truck, no PA. EMI stumped up for the album, but....we begged 'em. To get out there, hype the bastard thing. They said no more dough till they recoup from sales.' His face. *Watcanyado?* 'We have to get back.' The crits really dug *Choice Cuts,* their new LP, he said. 'Glenn's talked Sitmar into free passage. Contra-deal. Our end, we promo their liners, get the kids in. We sail next week.'

The Masters, before that year was out, would be rent asunder. Many are called...

'Got a ciggie'? More whisper than voice. Rehearsal, Headquarters, midday.

'Sure', I said. She took two.

'Your own set first, then back the floorshow,' Hamish had said. Headband did a lot of this after that Drum deal, with singers from the eastern states, the freight for their full bands deemed too exy.

Wendy Saddington's hair, bigger than the rest of her. Monster Afro. Eyes, more kohl than Cleopatra. All baubles, bangles and beads. *Kachink, gjangle,* every time she moved.

'So,' I said. 'Got your charts?'

'Got my what?' *Nada.* Unheard of in Headband's collective experience. 'Can we just start with a slow blues?' She almost smiled. 'I don't like fast ones.'

'Okay. What keys you sing in?'

'Fucked if I know. What key is this'? Sang a line. '*Gotta find me a way, to get some peace of mind...*' Fuck. *Here was voodoo.* I scrambled round the keyboard.

'We're in C, boys,' I said.

'So can you play a twelve bar intro, and then I'll come in?' A question, unsure of itself.

'As you wish, mademoiselle', said Joff. 'One and a two and a' *blat blat blat bop bup boom,* to bring us in. Wendy, moving now, into our groove, shifted from wallflower to top dog in the yard. For the intro verse, a Mauri solo. A crying at midnight sound, not quite like anyone else. 'We Finns are very special people,' he'd often remind us. And sometimes he was right. Like now. Wendy came in, the first line, as per blues custom, repeated on the fourth chord. Then hit the word *peace.* Shot up an octave, into the clouds. Into *space.* Same all the way through, on words like *soul* or *kill* or *please.* The hair on the nape of my neck, up like a hound's. *I wanted to howl like one.*

'Take a break, eh?' I said at song's end. We needed one. 'You smoke?'

'Fuck, man,' said Wendy, a husky chuckle with it. 'Thought you'd never ask.' We shared the reefer round as we mapped a set list. She hadn't brought one of them either. 'Nina? Nina Simone? Into her?' Was I ever. 'Bessie Smith? Aretha?' She liked what we liked. Dylan too, *Just Like Tom Thumb's Blues*. 'You excited, Peter?' It must have shown.

'I am, Wendy, I am,' I said. Our first go off the chain, to play the music we prayed to.

That night the joint's jammed. Word had got round. *Not by mouth, but on the wind.* To open, a set of Headband's originals. And then...

'Brothers and sisters, boys and girls, beings from other planets and cosmic groovers,' from sometime Melbourne promoter, poet, moocher and scenester Adrian Rawlins, compere at Myponga and other festis, now based here. 'Welcome to the stage, the Goddess of groove, the Boudicca of the blues, the Queen of the Nile of soul - *Wendy Saddington!*'

Wendy blew the sky away. She set us free.

'I hear you're well-fleshed,' he said. As in versatile. Like Wendy, flown in as a solo. 'Happy to gig wherever fate and the four winds decree.' Jeff St John in a wheelchair now. By choice. 'Frees up my fists, not full of walking sticks, so I can make with the chair dancing.' For this force of nature, spina bifida no encumbrance.

Jeff's charts, superfine, by John Bird or Barry Kelly, pianists in his band Copperwine. Their recent album, *Joint Effort*, denied what it deserved. 'Its genres diverse served only to confuse, you see,' he said. 'The critics raved, but alas, whinged as well.' His favourite, the nong who'd said *Will the real Jeff St John please stand up?*

It was a blinder show. Leon Russell's *Hummingbird* a standout. *Big Time Operator* and *Teach Me How To Fly*, Jeff's biggest hits to date. *Parchman's Farm*, that Mose Allison gem, Ray Sharpe's classic *Linda Lu*. Brought down every brick on the block with funk workout *Don't Get Me Wrong*.

And that act! Rode it like a motorbike, pulled wheelstands and wheelies in that buggy. Jeff claimed a four-octave range, but I'm calling five. Six. He taught us how to fly.

THIRTY

The tour, backed by Sammy Lee, Sydney nightlife bigshot and all the ugly that came with that. Deep Purple, Free and Manfred Mann tore up the night at the Apollo Stadium, Frats the support. But stories about, of Manfred's manager bashed in Melbourne by goons packing shooters. And Manfred and band, tonight, hiding from these very mutts in the parklands rear of the Adelaide Zoo. Free, my guess, seeking refuge from those same warbs when that enchanted foursome of Rodgers, Kossoff, Fraser and Kirke came through the door.

'Boz told us to look you up, mate. Mind if we sit in?' Old mate Boz, by now with King Crimson. Me, a solo piano job that night, Bogarts wine bar. Patrons here couldn't believe it. Backline there, amps, drums, so Free and I played our boots off, hot, loose blues, an hour or so. Under a sickle moon that night in May, one of the gigs of my life.

Big Daddy's Discotheque, the biggest room midtown. Headband could fill it from here to the last of time, I told Bob Lott. We'd be promo'd to Pluto and back, I said, via Vince in *Go-Set* and *The News,* TV spots on *Move,* and a slot on Seven's upcoming Good Friday Telethon, for disabled kids, the whole town tuned in. *Sold*. Thursdays, Fridays, Saturdays, from late to way past that.

'Quick sticks, boys. Time's on the move,' all we ever heard from Jimmy Popov, or Popoff, maybe Russian for *shithead*. The manager at Daddy's a real wide boy, spiv, hustler, take your pick from the board. Did a lot of local radio or telly, to bignote his head off, a delusion that he was a showbiz personality.

We did three months there. But around month two, Jimmy stopped paying us. Come the third, he skipped town, with around five large of ours and like sums owed to others. Bob Lott, a decent rep to protect, not into sending the boys around. Ain't that a shame.

Meantime, Hamish had Headband on high rotation at all the Headquarters, his 'private adventures' as Bob Lott called them with a smile. And we're playing high schools lunchtimes. Memory frail and faded, but may have been a Dunstan state government initiative. Soon, five of those a week, and in that same zone, high school socials, formals, come evenings. One night, this kid, fourteen, tops, came to the back of the school hall with an overture that she root the four of us on the spot. Um, *pass*.

Now and then, we were booked direct, as in told that we were on, refusal an option best not entertained, for bikie shows out in the scrub. Well, the price was right. Rich as King Farouk, these funpigs. Players in the speed and acid game, my guess. You played all night. On into the breakfast shift if they said so.

'Thirty dollars. Weekly. *Cash money*,' said Hamish. Our wage, skinny, even in the dollars of '71, on a promise that the rest of all that dough we were pulling in was destined for investing in our future beyond the South Oz border, those far and golden uplands. He'd swing by the gallery Fridays with my two pay packets, plus one each for Chris, Mauri and Joff. Hamish preferred it this way. You see, Fraternity would troop into the Grape office every week, all seven strong, for *their* pay. Bruce Howe and Mick Jurd, the bandleaders, not keen on playing often, so often at odds with Hamish, and each week bearing fresh flotillas of complaints and demands, for new gear and such. Not big on something for nothing, Hamish would counter with unkind assessments of their work ethic. *Where are all these new songs I keep hearing about?*

It all started to send Bon mad. They did tour. Hamish insisted. These, booked on his trips interstate, his confabs with industry heavies there, to grease the wheels for both our bands. But Frats only ever did two or so nights in Melbourne or Sydney. Perth once. A gig at Surfers cut short, Frats run out of town off Bon's dig at some cops who'd forced them to cut their volume. But Headband played twice or more a day, six days a week. 'Frats, fuck. All show and no go,' said Bon one day, confiding in Mouse and I. 'Ain't no fun waiting round to be a millionaire.'

'Hamish says England,' said Bon. I couldn't help but disagree. The US, a readymade market for that country funk Frats did so well. The UK, toxic, endless short-lived fads dealing death to last week's darlings. A suicide mission. But Frats, hampered by Bon's pot bust. The US wouldn't grant a visa, the assumption. Yet he'd later tour there with ACDC, so who knows? I recalled for Bon my own time in London, the fate of the Masters, the Easybeats, the Twilights. 'Don't do it,' I said. Bon told Frats. Deaf ears.

'You *cunt!* Wrong fucking *chord!*' Bon had me to a Frats rehearsal one day, I think just to prove what he'd told me. *It never bloody stops, you know.* Mid-song, Bruce Howe stopped dead, stomped over, belted organist John Bisset. Bon flashed me that wide-eye popstare of his. *See what I mean?* Weird. This crew, forever upstairs on the mushrooms, the dacca, the hash, yet so prone to this. Maybe down to the lagoons of booze they necked along with all the other. Vince always viewed Bon as drifting through life 'in a dreamworld' known only to him. Me, I suspect they all were.

'Oh, fuck. Here we go,' he says. We're headed for a Frats gig one night, Largs Pier. On foot, the pub six blocks thence, no parks closer. *'Hey, Bon!'* Three of them. Visigoth beards, heads like Old Norse trolls, Stone Age mullets. *'Our girls are a bit keen on you.'* They bar our path. 'Yeah, righto, boys,' he says, half their height and bulk. 'Who's first?' He's all street fighter. They saw just how ready he was. Dropped off. We walked straight through them.Happened often to Bon, and didn't always end so well. Some days he'd hand out beatings, to dopes too dumb to jerry they couldn't fight. Of those who could, on occasion, different outcome. Bon, crazybrave. A handy quality. And a fatal flaw.

THIRTY-ONE

Midway through our first year, Vince wrote up Headband in *Go-Set*. Vytas took individual pix of us, after the Beatles' *Let It Be* cover. Vince egged it up to billyo. Each of us a prodigy, ours a supergroup. Stablemates to Frats, and so, like them, the way Vince told it and sold it, soonest for global acclaim.

CBA booked us far and wide now. Beyond Adelaide, a thousand pubs, clubs, town halls, ballroom to bloodhouse. To Whyalla, *the Alla*, the Mauri Berg Lands. To Port Lincoln. Port Pirie. Port Augusta, *The Gutta*. Mundulla, Millicent, Mount Gambier, *The Mount*. Riverland towns. Berri, Renmark. Closer to home but no less mulga feral, Murray Bridge.

'Long haired poofters' still the descriptor of choice for travelling minstrels out in the donga. *'Play somethin' we know. Or we'll fuckin' do ya,'* before we even started. To hose 'em down, four on the floor blues, loud as dayglo. For the kids in the town halls, chartbusters off the radio. Our blooding, this, for future battlefields. 'You don't measure up, Melbourne crowds will turn to stone. And Sydney, well, they'll rip your heads off.' Thus was the word on the wire.

Chris Bailey near got Headband axed to chunks on these bush runs. Women swooned for him. *'Whatyoufugginlooginat?'* from their droog boyfriends. Our roadies, Paul Hille and Greg Rosman, tough as a life sentence, would stand in front of us, something of steel close to hand to club down stage invaders should need emerge. Our Drongo Squad.

And to charm the orcs and balrogs, comics in our ranks. Chris, king of the one-liners, our own private Henny Youngman, while Joff had other tricks. He used to wear a huge sombrero onstage, like you get at the Royal Show. Under that, his secret weapon. For a big finish to one of Joff's blue jokes, he'd rise and bow, doff the sombrero. Then with his other hand he'd lift off his hairpiece, flashing them a full frontal nude of his hair-free dome. They never saw it coming. Laughed till they near soiled themselves.

We only got to play our originals now and then. One such gig, with Blackfeather, featuring their guitar wizmeister John Robinson. Wendy Saddington on the bill that day too, with Blackfeather backing the Big W at this June '71 stir for Alex Innocenti at Glenelg Town Hall, those headliners from across the border plus most every band in town. A dry gig, no liquor license, so the crowd, and not a few of the players, all the way *spaced*. Tripping on Strawberry Fields, Purple Pyramids, Brown Dots. Or ripped, courtesy of black hash, hash oil, Buddha sticks, homegrown. Or both.

Your underground promoters round Australia bunged on these dry shindigs in town halls and such, as there were few stages for 'head' acts to play. Then came the hot winds of change, the new gold rush of pub rock.

THIRTY-TWO

'Biggles! I need that hippie band of yours.' Ron T's lined up fellow Redlegs supporter Robyn Archer to write and record *The Ballad Of Phil Carman*, of Norwood's star player. A private pressing, 'three hundred singles to flog to the fans,' said Ron. At Max Pepper's studio, Robyn lobs with a leg in plaster, on crutches. Wouldn't say how or why, true to trouper custom, to drip-feed that aura of enigma and mystery. The B side, *Waltzing Matilda*. The footy hoons would love it, Robyn said. 'And public domain, Ron, down to its age. No royalties payable.' Mr T's kind of music.

'Forget it, Ron.' The credit *Robyn Archer* on the label would boost sales, as Robyn had played the Redlegs Club many times and gone over a bomb, but taking coin from The Man for *this*, well, the way Robyn saw it, that precious *demi-monde* cred would be sullied beyond repair. And Ms Archer, made of iron even harder than Ron. So it came to pass that *Madam X* was settled upon as the artist credit. Sold big. Ron paid us a tasty flat fee for the sesh, but that sales gravy boat, all his. You bet.

'Same as Ziggy and the King's. How about that?' To Hamish, it was a line of easy credit. The record deal he's winkled Headband, a repayable loan, really, as they all be, so we're all at sea in iceberg season if we flop. But such prospect, surely inconceivable. For this label was a major. *Latest releases from RCA. From Elvis and Bowie and Headband.*

Scratch My Back, the first Berg/Beagley number chosen for rendering unto vinyl. Lyrics by Mauri, the only head in the band whose primo lingo's not English. Music down to Yours Truly, our sole inhouse jazznik. No wonder it sounded like no beast of this earth.

'A chamber recital?' said Joff. 'Oh, I don't know. Is there pizza?' A self-imposed *indoctrination program,* Chris called it. My brainwave. For Headband, some schooling. Example, a concert of JS Bach cello suites at the Elder Con at Adelaide Uni. 'All the prog bands steal from old Johann Sebastian,' my counsel. 'And they're coining it in.' We even learned a Bach prelude to play live, *because Jethro Tull did,* it was pointed out, but never got around to field-testing it. Why, lost in the stone haze from some hollowed-out carrot repurposed as hash chillum some hazy day.

At a choral recital I dragged them along to, among the Handel and Mozart, a barbershop quartet bit, *Shine On Harvest Moon* or some other evergreen. Inspired me to write the music for *Headsong,* some other lyrics of Mauri's. 'Can you do anything with these, Pedro?' I persuaded Mauri and Joff to sing, a first for them, with Chris. Three vocal parts, just piano to light the way. Hamish wanted things *far out,* he said, to market Headband as unique and compelling. So we took our sailboat and hotted it up. For space travel.

'You play too many chords, Pedro. I can't keep up.' Mauri a self-described *rough boy from the 'alla,* forged from the blues and Finnish folk songs. Me, a jazzer. No such animal as more than you need. Imperative, then, I said, that we check out Glenn Heinrich, vibraphone and sax player, his quartet, and Schmoe and Co. Schmoe, born Sylvan Elhay, tenor sax, sidekicks Geoff Kluke bass, Fred Payne trumpet, Dean Birbeck drums, Grahame Conlon, guitar. Like Headband, they played the Barr-Smith Lawns or the Refectory at Adelaide Uni, or at Flinders Uni, booked by the student unions there. Or bistros, Roaring 20s themed setups of the time like Dillingers. And that fleet of wine bars like the Pink Pig that came and went like the Whitlam government.

And local jazzers did all-night stirs at Carclew, a heritage-listed Federation mansion with a witches' hat tower on Montefiore Hill. At 'Swinger' at the ritzville Hotel Australia, we checked out Paragon, a jazz-funk outfit. All this to blend swags of styles, to spin up new sonic stars.

'Record co rules,' said Hamish. 'Studios here not up to it, they say.' Daddy Cool, the Aztecs, Russell Morris, The Masters, Farnham, had all tracked Number Ones at Armstrong's. And so whence must go Headband, to this hit factory in South Melbourne.

Midnight, Friday gigs done, we hit the road. A big Holden Statesman de Ville from City State, Hamish at the wheel. Eight hours via that deathtrap two-lane east, then the Coburg to South Melbourne hellcrawl.

At Armstrong's, three hours to track *Scratch My Back* and its B side, *Musical Man*. Quite terrible, we realised when we heard the playbacks, but all we had in the tank then to pass as a single. Then home, eyes out for cops. That night's gigs won't play themselves. *Go.*

THIRTY-THREE

'So, Peter. I need an arranger.' Alan Slater calling from Derek Jolly's studio. The brief, jingles, for radio and TV. Hillsides of them. Slater's paid top dollar, but I said *yes* before we even got to that.

'Well, it beats cutting cane.' Freddy Hampton laid down his machete one day and made south to follow that dream. In Sydney, cut some 45s for the Spin label. Now, a face around Adelaide, two solo singles out on Derek Jolly's Gamba label, a band called Trik, and at Slater's, king of the jingle.

Way it went most days, Freddy played drums along with my piano track, then tracked the bass, me the Hammy. That done, his guitar and vocal. We cut hundreds of ads this way. Or to save time, Slater's hired Headband in full. We'd troop in between a lunchtime high school gig and that night's show. Work those mutts.

Radio station, 2ST, in the Southern Highlands of NSW, were after some station promos one day. Freddy away, so I thought *why not? 2ST from the mountains to the sea, 2ST is the one for me.*

Whisky wrote the words, dacca the music. 2ST ran them for years, no clue, nor their listeners, that it was Bon Scott. And likely never will.

Phil Cunneen played piano better than me, guitar and bass better than most. Phil's day gig, pianist for *Here's Humphrey,* the Nine kids' show. 'Down for the count, brother,' he croaked down the line. Flu, he said. 'No way I'm a starter tomorrow.'

Weird call, this job. All improv, fills and runs at the piano for Humphrey B Bear dancing, playing with his toys, doing dressups with non-bear co-host Patsy Biscoe. Inside the bear suit, Edwin 'Teddy' Duryea. A sweet man, Teddy, one of several Humphreys.

'The critics will be brutal, petal,' he said that first day. 'But fret not. They're just *jealous.*' I did a sward of *Humphrey* after that, whenever Phil was indisposed. Just one thing I could never got my head around. The Big H, role model to littlies, *wore no pants*, I pointed out to Teddy one day.

'Yes, dear. The job has its perks.'

'It's footy season, that's why.' Vince calling, and the news, that kind that be sent to try us. Headband, booked for a spot on *Move* tomorrow. But the show had been shifted from Saturday mornings to two PM a few months back. With half the town at the ovals across town watching the games live, the other half shouting at them at home on a rival network, *Move* had stopped rating. 'So they took it out and shot it this morning,' said Vince. One thing clearer by the day if Headband was to survive into '72. Time to blow this town and get over yonder's wall.

THIRTY-FOUR

'You'll never work up here again,' the last words he ever said to me. It was Headband's first real tour, sunny Q, the Playroom at Surfers and the Coolangatta Hotel. We're on a bill with Blackfeather, and before that, just south of there, the Tweed Heads Hotel with Tamam Shud. Six weeks all up, and that shifty fuck Dayman, fallen king of the Adelaide dance halls, running the show here on the Goldie, having bolted from his empire Melbourneside, his stable of stars there from Normie Rowe to the Purple Hearts featuring a young Lobby Lloyd, most likely stiffed out of fortunes.

Same old MO here from Ivan The Terrible. Five minutes to showtime, last night at the Gatta, we're still unpaid for the three-week run and he's about to bail. *Punters a bit thin on the ground, Peter.* We'd packed every gig. *You'll get it when I get it.* Well, I got it before we went on. It was my counter-offer. The cabbage, all of it, *now,* or we walk. No bands tonight, cut to empty room, pub's boss boiling over.

That dance of the brolgas, a sour end to a great run and a rolling party, staying in a fine old Queenslander that Dayman owned there. The Shuds had rolled in toting a jumbo bag of Mullum heads deluxe. Our first and last Bananaland swing, a pile of fun.

Some unfun too. A pipe after the gig one night left us paralysed, on the outskirts of a freakout. Then Mauri went a greygreen shade, broke out in a flopsweat, shivering, a buzzing sensation in his skull, he said. Locked himself in the pisshouse, head between knees, gone for three eternities before we thought to check on him, all of us next door to comatose off that reefer. A near-dead *Yeah* through the dunny door as to whether he was OK. That bag of green, spiked. Hospital-grade skag, most likely by the seller, a dud crop dosed up with a blast. Let the buyer beware.

'Frats are in it so the Heads should be too,' said Vince. Back home now, at our weekly pow-wow at the House of Hamish. 'Daddy Cool would shit it in but they aren't starters is the mail.' He meant Hoadley's, their annual Battle Of The Sounds, swag and treasure to first past the post. Hamish not keen, that bubblegum scene not a good look for our head fanbase. Yet Vince talked him round, all that dosh to fund those dreams should we take the flag. Two shots at the title for a sack of cash, free studio time at Armstrong's, and *air fares to LA or London*.

The South Oz heats, July 7, Thebarton Town Hall. Third-rate covers bands from all over the state made the scene. Chris B summed it best. 'A swarm of shitpots and each a grand delusion.' Backline provided, sub-par. Headband left our amps and drums at home, as ordered, and bombed. Frats brought their own, a crowd too. Stacked the room. *We have a winner*. Took out the Grand Final over Sherbet and Jeff St John as well, Frats, at Festival Hall in Melbourne a few months down the line. No inkling that this win would be a player in their undoing.

THIRTY-FIVE

'Well, I've got *this* hill of shit. And *he's* got a Steinway.' Vince and Hamish had finagled Headband the Adelaide support for the star's first Oz tour. At soundcheck at Memorial Drive, the feeble twinkle of my rinky dink Hempenstill, exposed and shamed on the big concert PA, and about to be to the three thousand who'd be here tonight. Headband's rep trashed. *In front of Elton John.*

We headed backstage. Often, back then, supports, no dressing room, or a Sunliner caravan with nothing in it. Why would this be any differen…'Boys! Come in!' Elton waves us into *his* quarters. 'Can I get you anything?' I scope the room for the rider. 'Fancy a cuppa?' *Tea and biscuits. That's it.* And gets the billy on himself, reefs out tea bags. We meet his drummer Nigel Olsson, bassist Dee Murray. And then, my voice within, *fuck it.* 'Hey, Elton. Can I use your Steinway?' My bandmates' faces, *fuck, Peter, don't…*'By all means, my man! Be my guest. I hate those electric pianos.'

It was ten minutes into our set. The PA died, *glomp.* Backline too. No amps or vocal mics, naught but the cold silence of empty air. *Except the Steinway,* still fanging out through the front of house, bright and clear. *So.* I decided to rip out some instrumentals while the crew scuttled round trying to revive their dead black Stonehenge. *Button Up Your Overcoat,* a number from the 1920s, the style of those old English pub singalongs. *Elton will get it.* The crowd, a few laughs, a clap at the end. But the PA, *still* kaput. So I rolled into some Thelonious, *Blue Monk.* They heard it as a blues and dug it. PA still out cold, so into *I Remember April,* learned from Wally Lund. I'm almost at the end when the PA belched, *gadoompf,* out of its coma. Elton's crew let Headband finish our set- most wouldn't- and we did our hometown proud.

'Grace under pressure, Peter! Well done, that man!' Elton, all smiles, giving us all an arms-out clap. 'Commendable. Commendable.' No fruity frillies back then, he's dressed as per the cover of his live album, *17-11-70. White jeans, green T shirt, satin bomber jacket,* memory whispers to me. A big star on the shirt, for such is he. Thanks, Mr John.

With Headband, the plan was we'd be the other half of the Fraternity show. In the end, didn't go that way. But that first year, quite a few such gigs, at the dry discos. By September of '71, as Vince eulogised in *Go-Set,* these near extinct, from the day the drinking age dropped and the bands swarmed across to the pubs. His Headquarters foursome Hamish put to the sword too. The few survivors, like the Princeton Club and Combine at Marion Shopping Centre, their fuddy dress regs, *ties essential,* along with being boozeless, twin turnoffs. No matter who they put on, Farnham, the Masters, these last of them struggled and withered, relics of times bygone.

Yet Hamish still bunged on one-offs here and there, a thumb in the teen dollar pie. October long weekend of '71, 'Battle Rock', a Sunday at Elizabeth's Octagon. From Melbourne, Russell Morris, huge then, and Brian Cadd, big off his days in The Groop and with Glenn Shorrock in Axiom. Frats, Headband to open. Compere, Vince, who jumped in for a duo vocal with Bon for *Little Queenie.* Those two damn near stole the show.

The Monday holiday, at Glenelg Town Hall, Hamish called 'Twilight Rock Expression.' Frats, Headband, Red Angel Panic. Openers, Captain Thunder and Ilo. The 'Twilight' bit, the early start and finish, this a school night.

And Hamish booked local halls to sell Frats and the Heads to the teens of the bush. One such, the Rivoli Theatre in Berri, South Oz riverland, an old cinema. Not so bad. Dry show, so all the town baboons convinced we'd come to fuck their sheilas and must die, gone to the pub to belt each other purple instead.

Bon liked these Frats-Heads bills. 'Means I get to hang with your crew,' he said, meaning Headband. Frats forever on the bicker and moan. The Heads, peaceniks, mutual respect, plenty ganja. 'The Green Peace reigneth,' as Chris had it.

It was the last of '71. Five nights, the Largs Pier and the Bridgeway, Pooraka. Headband did the Pier first, then made for Pooraka. Frats, at the Bridgie, headed for the Pier. Our pirate ships in the night passed halfway between. Both pubs, packed as hell below.

They say it went for three days. The two pubs, stoked with the result, shouted us a barbecue up at Frats HQ at Aldgate. Fully staffed bars, boundless grog, butchers doing bulk deliveries. A high time had. Or so we were told. For Headband, business as usual, booked right up to New Years Eve. And further.

'I worry about you, Peter.' Bon's wicked twinkle in his eyes. 'All skin and bone. Here. Breakfast of the stars.' He cracked a bottle as the bus eased out on to the road. Fuckit. Got stuck in. Today, a ten AM start. For *musicians*. Rally at Grape, to board the bus that Hamish has bought for Frats to tour in. Only Hamish would stage a one day festi on New Years Day, the nation both feet in the grave from Godzilla-sized hangovers. But kids had bought tickets, so the show must go off. 'Snap Crackle And Rock' Hamish badged it, chasing that teen dollar, Berri again. Three hours drive, or three bottles of Johnnie Red. Next door to paralytic by the time we made the site, off that and the spliffs I circulated. Limbs gone to water. Heads, up where the clouds make way for the stars.

'It's too hot to fuck, even,' someone said. Bon, chuckling, *nah, never too hot for that*. Forty degrees. Played shirtless, tray of a truck. Tarp over the back half, so shade for drummers and amps. The rest of us, baked red and aglow by sundown. Our set, well, different. Sailed by stars only we could see.

THIRTY-SIX

'You're not doing this one, Peter.' Hamish, backing Meadows Technicolour Fair, sequel festi to Myponga in the summer of '72. Again, a showcase for Frats. Overseas acts, folkies this time, Tom Paxton, Mary Hopkin, and vapid pop combo Edison Lighthouse, their one hit, *Love Grows,* two years back. But fab locals. Spectrum, Tamam Shud, Blackfeather. Vytas, a set of sitar. Chasing the weirdo coin this time too, Hamish. Rock Masses for Jesus freaks and other cults from across the spiritual spectrum.

Across the border, another festi that same weekend, Headband to fly the Grape battle flag there. Up against Billy Thorpe and The Aztecs, Lobby Lloyd's Wild Cherries, Chain, that steamy funk of Max Merritt And The Meteors. Heavy company, but road-hard and primed, we'd slay 'em at Sunbury.

Well, they must have thought so, too. We'd just loaded up Big Red, our Hamish-provided Ford Transit van in shade of cherry tomato, when word came. Bumped. Too many acts, too few timeslots. *Bummer, man, but what can you do?*

Sunbury '72 made a star of Thorpie all over again, and created a host of others, via the album and film. Yeah. We got that close.

'I got him exclusive. Only gig in town.' Out here on tour, but no Adelaide show. So Hamish picked up the phone and one pot o' gold later, John Mayall, king of British blues, was on his way. Clapton, Peter Green, McVie and Fleetwood from Fleetwood Mac and Mick Taylor from the Stones had all served in Mayall's Bluesbreakers. Based in LA now, Mayall, packing a new A Team he called Jazz Blues Fusion. The gig, Adelaide Uni Commencement Ball. Supports, Captain Matchbox and Headband. In '72, Still a major draw, Mayall, so a sold out show. *Jackpot.*

We had a new original, *Stay With Me,* Black Sabbath meets Deep Purple under a blood moon. The mob went full bananas when we road-tested it that night. Another, *Children's Dream,* a Uriah Heep style of deal. They ate it up and howled for more.

'Yeah, go home and listen to the record, chum.' Pure Mayall, to punters calling for his latest radio hit, *Room To Move.* Ambled on in shorts and a harmonica belt, no compere's intro. Bid his players kick off with a wave of his hand.

But how about that band! Freddy Robinson's guitar took off the tops of our heads. Pre-Mayall, he'd survived those two thunderballs of Chicago blues, Little Walter and Howlin' Wolf. Blue Mitchell on trumpet, late of Ray Charles, Cannonball Adderley, others. Bass ace Larry Taylor, ex-Canned Heat, had freaked at how long the flight from LA was, and bolted. So Mayall roped in Putter Smith, ex-Monk, Ellington, all *that* pantheon.

They split soon as they were done. Gonesville when we rolled backstage to see if they wanted to head out for a blow. Maybe had a pre-dawn redeye back to LA. I found myself wishing I did too.

'Do we have to?' By '72, the Hoadley's Battle, near to gone the way of all things. But, said Hamish, a win meant riches to sing our dreams to life. So yes, we had to.

We won the South Oz heats by default. Many gave the Battle a swerve now, an event grown tired and so more or less ignored by the media, unhip to the point of terminal. Still, we're headed for the finals in Sydney, a toe in the moat round *that* castle of glory.

'Hit and split won't even touch the sides,' said Hamish. Meantime, this was the year we would take Melbourne, off his deal with Bill Joseph, boss cocky at the Australian Music Booking Organisation, an outfit he headed up with assist from Gary Spry and Sadie Sambell. *The Rajah,* they called him, ran near all Melbourne. But for Headband, no three night stands. 'You *live* there,' decreed Hamish. 'Three months, till the whole town has seen you. Can't miss.'

It meant changes. Roadie Paul Hille, just married, and a spouse unkeen on factory-fresh other half twelve weeks AWOL in rock 'n' roll Babylon. Greg Rosman, no such quibbles. And Tooley from the Pier, keen to jump into Paul's Dunlop Volleys. The mad bastard.

'Hang about, cock. I'll go up and 'ave a Captain, any bodies to shift before I let you in.' Laughing but not joking, this little Cockney geezer Ernie, concierge, Majestic Private Hotel, Fitzroy Street, St Kilda. Our rooms redefined *grot* and *grotty*. But each its own bathroom, a deal-sealer for its junkie and hooker clientele. Balconies too. 'Sunshine. For plants,' I pointed out to Chris. Joff and Mauri in the scuzzcave adjacent and the aroma of Brut 33 all over. Smackies loved it. Saved having to bathe.

Street crime here not out loud like the Cross. Festered in blue shadows. A week in, I'm walking a back lane one day, a short cut back to the Majestic. At the rear of the roughest pub on Fitzroy Street and a pioneer gay club adjacent, a fella loading slabs of Melbourne Bitter into the boot of a cop car. Two uniforms, blue overcoats, keen eyes on proceedings. Well. If that's what it took to keep the nightlife lifing, the choogle choogling,...

Yeah, the Kilda. The Gatwick, a pub for madmen only. Skagheads, crims, speed freaks, the homeless. Up the street from the Gat, in a past life, the ritzville George Hotel, now badged the Wintergarden, dressed these days in signage that made plain its business.

TITS. GETCHA GEAR OFF. AO. MORE SKIN TO THE ACRE.

Over time, its name changed again and again, each a fresh dressing on a wound. Seaview Ballroom, Crystal Ballroom, or just Ballroom. Another great ruin here, The Ritz, nowadays a hive of pimpcaves by the hour, to bring johns to the boil. Our faces, betraying misgivings we dare not voice. We put it from our minds. Here was a town needed conquering.

'Bill Joseph,' he said. Thrust a hand at me. His office, La Trobe street. 'How hard you like to work, Peter?' He answered his own question. From Week One, The Rajah, called such off his Sri Lankan heritage, liked his talent to slave as hard as he did. That meant two to three gigs. Per day. Saturdays, four, five, early arv to Sunday sunup. Some, in St Kilda, the Espy, the Esplanade Hotel. The Prince Of Wales, or *POW* as in *prisoner of war*, locals tagged it. And the Greyhound, corner of Carlisle and Brighton. Across Melbourne, on bills with Daddy Cool, Spectrum, Country Radio, Tamam Shud, Madder Lake, Blackfeather, Company Caine. And Mackenzie Theory. The Theory, from another place. Out past Andromeda at least.

North of St Kilda, we did the Station Hotel, on the level crossing at Prahran. Also here, Garrison Disco on High Street. Citywise, Berties, corner of Spring and Flinders, the Thumpin' Tum on Little La Trobe, or the far east at the Village Green at Mulgrave. As did Chain, the La De Das, Band Of Light, the Dingoes, and that other host of bands, the forgotten who fell at the first fusillade.

'Well, only Thorpie, Chain and Lobby play here, mate. The rest are too fuckin' scared.' *Now you tell me.* At the White Horse Hotel, Nunawading, bar manager says it's a sharpie pub. The *original* sharpie pub. 'Not to worry. Just play what Thorpie does.' He shrugged. 'Or call an ambulance.'

It was here that the sharpie chant 'suck more piss' was conceived. Fights every night. You played slaughterhouse blues or got your skulls caved in. Mauri could eat Lobby Lloyde alive on the guitar, but heresy to say so this side of the border.

The Ferntree Gully pub was worse, the sharps here narky from the off. Our crime, their females assessing our Chris B as *a bit of orright*. Greg Rosman, flying the sound board, went close to being bashed that night.

Jumped into Big Red and fanged away just in time, a mob of sharps in pursuit. He acquired a shooter after that, too easy round Melbourne in those days. Stashed it in Big Red, loaded with saltpeter. It was never deployed. Well, as far as I know.

'What the fuck is *ICELAND?*' To far Ringwood the Rajah sent us, one arv a week. Live bands, the Rajah had convinced them, would pull oceans of surly teens to this skating rink. It was some trip, serenading kids doing circles on the ice. And weekday lunchtimes, high schools, Balwyn to Camberwell, Fitzroy to Frankston, Doncaster to Dandenong. 'Well done, fellas,' said a teacher one day. 'Kids here today we haven't seen in weeks.' Oh, well. Hard-won means to good end, the only way to look at it. And with The Rajah, never had to chase it. Earn, on time, up front, full whack. A rare beast.

'Well, it bombed.' For our fresher single *Scratch My Back,* profound indifference beyond Adelaide. A bawlout from RCA, and our task now, 'to take the s back out of hit,' said Chris. Our second single for RCA, *Land Of Supercars,* tracked at Armstrongs. Ninety percent Mauri's, but he decreed a Berg-Beagley-Bailey-Bateman credit for our new 45, so lootsville all round should it chart big. Same for the flip, *Oh, How I Miss The Country.*

Supercars, nods to progmeisters Focus and Yes, but a four on the floor beat any goose could groove to. This, to hook radio airplay. For the heads, a middle section instrumental, Mauri peeling off notes from the fourth dimension, then a splash of jazz, my piano solo. *Oh, How I Miss,* more like The Band than The Band, from that other hemisphere of the prevailing winds.

Lo and behold, serious chart action. Back home, Barry Bissell, hipmost at the groovemost 5KA, pushed *Supercars* hard, as did other jocks from KA and AD. Vince Lovegrove to thank for that. 'Nothing to it,' he said when I did. Roved round town, he said, got people as stoned as he, and *then* played it to them. *Supercars* went alright in Melbourne too. Sydneyside, our guess, the payola sling too rich for the record co's blood. Only one way to fix that. A move that would change me forever.

THIRTY-SEVEN

'Married? *Eh?*' We're back in the hometown for some shows. Bon, yeah, *Bon*, the apex root rat, at the Town Hall registry, to Irene, they said. 'Yeah, she's a gas,' said Bon when we caught up. 'Too much. More like me than even me.' True enough. Bon and Irene, a mutual taste for Bazza Mackenzie comic strips, written by Barry Humphries, now out as books, *Bazza Pulls It Off* and *Bazza Comes Into His Own*. Banned in Oz, a hot item. The why of this union, well. Frats off to England, and soonish. Hamish said he'd stump up the fares for wives only, not squeezes. And so did they cast their dice.

'Can you come and have a squiz?' Bon had an old upright piano he'd bought for a hundred notes. Maybe to write songs on, I don't know. My appraisal, well. 'A box of shit.' Way out of tune, and five or six dead keys. My guess, Bon's planning to ask for lessons, but after my frank and brutal I heard no more.

'*Rock On,* it's called.' I ran into him back in St Kilda. Jim Keays now running a booking agency, and off to see his backer. 'Want to come?' Didn't want to go alone. Molly being Molly and all.

Casa Meldrum, flash as a rat with a gold tooth, a swish pad on Alexandra Avenue, South Yarra. Generous host, Molly. A drinkathon ensued. As like as not, Molly's on the con, but neither Jim nor I up for his brand of fun. Apart from *that*, Molly a mad keen Egyptophile, a monster collection of ancient artifacts here. I thought about putting in a word for Headband. Molly had a column in *Go Set*, was on the radio, telly on *Happening '72*, a useful public loudmouth to get onside. And he'd produced hits, *Smiley* for Ronnie Burns and Russell Morris with *The Real Thing*. But after all I'd heard, what Molly liked, and why, couldn't see him getting too amped up, short of Chris Bailey as sacrifice to his desires. And that, *not even for the glory of the regiment, Peter*, I pictured Chris declaring, so...

For Headband's first chomp at Sydney, Hamish lined up agent and manager Gene Pierson, at one time a pop star who'd crossed over when one too many singles ran out of go down the wrong end of the charts. Gene's domain as booker, the hotspots up the Cross and round the city. Owner, for public notice anyway, John Harrigan, a player round the Sydney scene since the early '60s. But other, unseen hands behind it all. Some, it was said, sticky with blood.

From memory, we did Chequers on Goulburn Street, the Whisky A Go Go up the Cross and a joint on King Street in town, Stagecoach Tavern. Huge room, this last one, all in red and gold. Provenance, I figured, Chinese. Turned out later on I was right. We knocked 'em flat and they dug us good.

From there, back doing Adelaide, and another go-round of the South Oz bush, to my horror. Felt strange, no Frats around, gone across the oceans mighty, to sweep England off its platform wedges.

'We were never in it.' Chris beat me to it. Near year's end, the Hoadley's finals, we're back in the smoke at Sydney's Hordern Pav. Sherbet's the chequered flag, all those squealing teenies they must have bussed in. Jeff St John, runner up. Our bronze medal, well, the tag of *Australia's third best pop group* one best left unutilised.

And it was around this time that news came from Hamish of RCA and Headband. The label a good fit for Elvis or Bowie, but no relish for building new acts. Their sales and royalty cheques, such as they be, cruised into Port Headband every three months, right on time. But the thrill was gone. I don't know who flicked who. Hamish had the cash to bet big, but few connections in the industry, and no real savvy as to how this game from a planet foreign was played. Best we bide awhile till the right ship came in. And so it did in time, 'round midnight and crewed by heavy players from Sydney's gangs of fallen angels.

THIRTY-EIGHT

'So this is where we take it from here,' said Hamish. Late '72, we're worn out and wondering what for. Two years yakka and becalmed on a sea of endless gigs, covers much of the time, for all tribes but our own. 'This will be the payoff,' he said. Now, as with Frats to England, Headband would move to Sydney. For good.

Hay, a township seven hours either way from Adelaide or Sydney. Yet Gene Pierson's people, *no worries, fella,* when Big Red conked and we called from the Caltex roadhouse. 'Ray sent me,' said the truckie when he rolled in from Sydney some hours later. I asked who Ray might be. He grinned. 'You'll find out.' He took off, Big Red on the truck tray. No lifts offered, so we crammed into Joff's car, the surviving half of our convoy.

We're told go straight there when we hit town, to unload Red. We're ratshit off two days of no sleep. But the vibe off Ray's truckie mate, well, best we comply.

'Welcome to Sydney, boys!' He thrust a bag of heads into Mauri's hand as he spoke. We're lugging into Chequers on Goulburn Street when he happens on the scene. 'Ray Arnold's the name.' Invites us into his shop adjacent, the Sydney Amp Centre. 'Plenty more where those beauties came from!'

'Boo!' In the lobby of this seedy flop next morning, none but Boo Boo Bronze, star stripper from La Belle. 'Same as you, Peter,' she said when I asked. 'Come to Sydney to seek my fortune.' She pointed at the ceiling.

'I'm upstairs. Penthouse. Catch you later,' she said. 'Can't keep the boyfriend waiting.'

Headband's first Sydney home, courtesy Gene Pierson. Lodge 44, New South Head Road, Edgecliff, a motel, its better days long passed. Next day, Boo's at my door. 'Hey, Peter. Get the boys together. My man wants to meet you.'

'Well, gentlemen.' A red silk smoking jacket draped about him, a face a smidge like Edward G Robinson from the old gangster flicks. 'You're working for me now,' he said as this big unit, his henchman or minder, poured whiskies. The little man in red raised his glass. 'So hang on for the ride.' He's twice Boo's years, mid-fifties, black hair dye the instant betrayer. 'You work for Gene. And Gene works for me.' He moved among us, shaking hands. 'Books all my rooms. You'll be working day and night with Gene on the job. He's a good boy.' A cold snap in his voice as he smiled. 'I hope you are too.' The goon pulled the door open. Meeting over. Well, then. We're working for Abe Saffron.

Chequers nightclub, a grunge cave once glam and glitz, when Sarah Vaughan, Sammy Davis Junior, Billy Eckstine had crooned and looned here. Chorus lines of dancers, tits and feathers, inhouse big band. Now, even their ghosts had bailed. Save one.

'Casey's the name. I'm the manager.' We only ever knew him as 'Mr Casey.' He still gussied up, in full tux, to greet punters, fetched them a full bow from the waist as they piled in at the spiral stairs just inside the entrance. The joint, still dressed in the frayed and faded of its last makeover. Dust-encrusted faux-Grecian columns, ditto busts on plinths. Wallpaper, dark brown and cream, that Seventies two-tone. The pattern, naked women.

'You're the best band that's ever played here!' At rehearsal there the afternoon of our first night, for some reason, we ran through *Fly Me To The Moon* and *Satin Doll*. It fair teleported Mr Casey back to the joint's glorious past. To *his* glorious past. A good and welcome omen. Others across those first nights, not so much.

It was the first of hundreds that followed, no less brutal. We've just knocked off at Chequers. Full house, same as most nights. Near us at the bar, a young rowdy, eighteen if that, arcing up a bit, but no biggie. Ray Arnold, slicked up in a Sydney doorman's tux, clocks the kid, storms over, clamps him in a headlock, free fist punching till the kid's face splits and spurts red.

'That was a bit rough, wasn't it?' Ray gave a us a lift home that night. Mauri couldn't process it. 'Mate,' says Ray, 'I've seen what these little pricks can do. That one, just as soon stick a knife in you. Deadset.' There was worse to come.

'Phil B Colson. How do.' At Chequers we did four nights a week, nine PM to eleven forty-five, with bands fore and aft of us. Sherbet, Band Of Light, The 69ers, Country Radio, Pirana, Ted Mulry Gang. Phil B's band Gunga Din on the *graveyard shift* he called it, twelve-thirty to two forty-five. 'Philby', we took to calling him. Sardonic, Philby, the chops of a stand-up comic, sizzling and bluesy on the guitar. And a night shift taxi driver, that Travis Bickle breed. We'd hire Philby to freight us between Chequers and Lodge 44 from time to time. None save Joff had a car here. Came to be fast friends, Philby and we.

'A bit of Sydney hospitality for ya.' Backstage, any night of the week, bags of Queensland heads, Thai Buddha sticks, caps of hash oil, a hash block like a house brick. 'You could lob that bugger through a jeweller's window,' said Ray, pointing with his baseball bat. Ray's amp and tackle shop next door, a handy front for wholesaling colossal cargoes of dope. Gave us unlimited free drinks as well. Ray and his crew did unspeakable violence to those he tagged as 'misbehavers,' but he treated us as friends, as he did the other bands. Wouldn't brook refusal of his generosity, so it was rock up, get stuck in, go on well and truly lit. Helped us deal with other stuff.

Ray's two offsiders, Big Tom and a mute giant they called The Deadly Dagger. I wasn't about to ask why. They kept spare jackets, dress shirts and bow ties close to hand, if blood should stain the broadcloth. Some they flung out on to Goulburn Street, maybe a kicking to go on with. *What's a few teeth?* Others, dragged out past the band room, head banging on the concrete and metal steps. Out of sight in the back lane, bashed to death's door. We'd go out for air between sets, and they'd be at our feet, bloodied but still breathing. Not this time. Not this one. This was a town out of control. And loving it.

'You won't just be playing Chequers.' Around eleven weeks in, Gene shifted Headband over to the Sydney Trocadero on George Street, gone to seed in extremis, soon to be demolished. The Troc, even unto its dying months, still ran a Ye Olde variety floorshow. We were doubled with a burlesque dancer, no other than Boo Boo. No full strip here, but damn near, Boo's bellydance of the seven veils. Well, six. Boo gave the four of us these finger cymbals that we clashed together in time to the routine. Our two weeks at the Troc, I think the last act to play there before they wiped it from the earth for a new Hoyts.

Gene booked us into the Whisky A Go Go, the Mandarin Club, Stagecoach Tavern in the city, and back at Chequers. The Whisky, Saturday and Sunday nights, when hell emptied out and all its devils made for the Cross. And daytimes now, we're dispatched to free outdoor shows sponsored by radio 2SM, or lunchtime gigs at all of Sydney's unis and tech colleges, from your sandstone statelies to redbrick battlers.

The World's Largest New Year's Eve Party, they called it. But for the Bungool festi on the Hawkesbury that last weekend of '72, the promoters didn't think to sling to the Baulkham Hills Shire Council, and water skiers a heavy lobby round these parts. No music lovers, they teamed up, took out an order and shut it down. Friday night cancelled, bands blown off, no pay.

Then someone noticed that the festi site was a registered campsite and *picnic ground.* Well, they'd paid to rent the site, so they re-invited all the bands to a three day picnic. The show chugged into life come Saturday arv, with whoever was still onsite. Wendy S, Blackfeather, Richard Clapton, Matt Taylor and more had all shot through.

No, it's all go, fellas, from Gene that Sunday morning, New Years Eve, after a three AM finish at the Whisky. We rolled into Bungool round midday, redeyed bleary. The goombahs at the gates, tooled up with dogs and shooters. Amenities, thin on the ground. And no first aid tent. 'So, then,' said Chris.'We are among savages.'

We'd been told we're on the bill for NYE, and we were. At *two PM*. They'd prophesied Sunbury hordes, tens of thousands. But just two large out there, scattered about in scalding shadeless heat.

After us, Jeff St John gave his all. Then, Band Of Light's live wire blues power. Later on, Sherbet almost hauled off and bashed, all that satin glam gear. The imbeciles down the front lobbed beer cans at the Sherbs, or maybe they were aiming at the moon and stars. Yet the band made it through to midnight, singer Daryl Braithwaite whomping out *Auld Lang Syne.* After twelve, the La De Das, Country Radio, Spectrum, to four AM, to dwindling numbers, the hoons passing out in Sandman panel vans and tents, sozzled and sizzled.

They tried to stage the third day's bill come New Years' morning. No takers. We fled with the rest. Had a gig that night, New Years Day, at the Manzil Room up the Cross, full of hardcores full of filthy biker crank. Sleep could wait. Our kind of people.

I don't know how he swung it, but Gene Pierson knew far better than Hamish that subterranean maze of record companies, all its minotaurs within. He'd cut a bunch of singles across his pop star years, for Philips, Festival and Infinity, and so was full bottle on who was who in the monster zoo.

'Same label as Clapton, The Who,' he said. 'And Hendrix before he left us for the next dimension.' Gene, bold and shrewd at a bargaining table, had scored Headband a mighty sack of gold from these moneylenders of the rock'n' roll temple. And not only that. Polydor wanted an *album*. A lot of record buyers, gone off singles these days, forsaken for LPs, as immersive trips to go with the dope du jour. Headband's originals, field-tested by now on a hundred gigfuls of punters zonked to murgatroyd on the three main drug groups. *Rolling*.

Ours was a full dance card most days, so only midnight to sunup free for the task now at hand. A year to complete an album, they said, and tipped us into the big EMI studios in Castlereagh Street to make it so.

'First things first, bandsmen.' David Fookes, late of Sydney band Freshwater, our producer. From his bag that first night, a brick of hash, dimensions of a Besser block. How we ever got that record finished, a mystery for the ages.

Our first Polydor single, *Country Lady*, just one chord, most of it. Melody with a bounce like the Beatles' *Two Of Us*. La la la la la la backing vocals, to appease the godkings of radio. *Stay With Me*, a hard blues driven by reggae rhythm for the B side.

'Boing boing boing boing...' Mauri overdubbed a jews' harp on *Country Lady*. I was dubious. Echoes of Rolf Harris or a John Williamson number, like *Old Man Emu*. 'Fret not, Peter. Australiana. Radio loves it,' said David. His, the last word on the subject. Down Under, even in the Seventies, producers were still vested by the Higher Powers with creative control.

And for sonic magic dust on *Lady*, David schlepped in a backup singer, from his band Freshwater, who told us of a sesh tracked a couple of months back over at ATA in Glebe, the soundlab Col Joye co-owned. 'For the Labor Party,' she said. David passed the pipe 'Backups?' Shook her head, took a toke. 'Nah. Lead.' Yep, Alison McCallum sang the hellfire out of *It's Time*. Backup singers Little Pattie, Jacki Weaver, Barry Crocker, Lynette Curran, Bert Newton, Graham Kennedy, Jack Thompson, Col Joye and the rest went alright too. Did they ever. The battle hymn that got Gough over the line. It was ace while it lasted.

THIRTY-NINE

Sydney was always meant to be a forever move prior to Headband slipping away to the UK or US on voyage of conquest, so three months along, we trucked in our dearest. *Sayonara* to Lodge 44 and the little man up on the roof.

For Mouse, Josh, little Lo and myself, our first Sydney home together a pad on Palmer Street, Darlinghurst. This, it fast became clear, a sex provider precinct. All genders, all hours, warpaint, sass and skin, the screech and wail of hand to hand combat, those turf wars of the midnight hour. Not there long, down to Mouse and a more fam-friendly find at William Street, Double Bay. Mauri and Janne rented a place elsewhere, likewise Chris and partner Wendy. Joff, no home but his mum's before Sydney, had fallen hard for Pandora Leeder, who worked at Chequers. They moved in with us.

'First thing Monday morning? What star cluster are these droogs from?' For *GTK*, AKA *Get To Know*, we're this week's feature act. This ten-minute treat, six-thirty PM weeknights, the ABC's once deadest timeslot now in the lush bloom of Aunty's best ever music show, then and for all time.

Meanwhile, back at half past sunup, the tech setup for filming at the Gore Hill studios, slow as an agent's cheque, an all-morning deal. At the other end of it, a short set, four songs, played live, to be broadcast over four nights. And on this day, a live audience, a new format *GTK* were trying out. Today, tenth formers and their teachers on the tiered seating.

GTK producers always insisted that bands do something other than their regular material. Our special one-off intro for *Country Lady*, Joff's idea. *Skippy The Bush Kangaroo* never sounded quite like this. And we chucked in a blues, Little Walter's *My Babe*, but at bebop speed, and with a scat singing solo from me, up and out from behind the piano. Ella I ain't, but it went alright.

'It's the biggest budget ever for an Australian album,' Gene told us. The brief from Polydor, a globe-friendly chartbuster. A big ask. UKside, prog rock the go, Floyd, Yes, Genesis, King Crimson. Across the Atlantic, Crosby, Stills, Nash and Young in all their permutations, Steve Miller Band, Eagles, Doobie Brothers. Our mission, to take fire from all these gods and make it as one. *Alright, then.*

More sessions now. We re-did *Land Of Supercars*, more ambitious arrangement this time round. *My Young Friend*, a ballad, Randy Newman vibe. Just a Chris vocal, me piano, some Hammond to season it up. In fact, every track on this long player that would come to be called *Song For Tooley* in honour of our beloved roadie, little resemblance to its companions. Headband's versatility, our mighty strength. And, way the wheel rolled in the end, our terminal debility. All those ears out there didn't know where to start.

Philip Morris, shooter from *Go-Set*, rocked into EMI one day. Took 'action shots' of us, headphones clamped on ears, bunched round the desk, at our instruments. They ran these with a yarn that Vince hyped up for *Go-Set* that we were tracking a double album. This, never on the cards, but no one had the hoopla down like the guy Bon called PhoneHead.

That was Vince, all hours, rolling up a scoob, receiver clamped under chin, that he might gabble on hands-free. This time, the industry buzzing loud over a thing that didn't exist. Mission accomplished.

'See? Like a UFO.' Hamish sent up Vytas to do the album's cover. As per norm, straight to it, not a word to a soul. A fifteen-inch speaker lying face down next to the soundboard in the control room one day, so Vytas took a blue biro and rendered it hovering in mid-air, as if an alien starship. Tooley was there that day, on the snooze, on his side, hands pressed under his head. Vytas captured that too, our loyal retainer in repose under a giant flying saucer in the sky, oblivious to the wonders of the universe, as most of us are.

Draft done, for three days Vytas scratched away now for the final cover art. Indian ink, brushes and nibs on plastic, not paper. He carved lines in it, the tiniest knife I ever beheld. Then drew in the ink, creating those interweaving, swirling patterns all over the cover. Same for the back, Tooley now aslumber here under a tree. The record co printed a pile of posters as merch, to sell at gigs, and as an insert, part of the LP package.

'Needs something,' said David. It's four AM, all ears to a playback of *Goodbye Mother Nature*. The *something*, it turned out, a hundred and twenty of them. Couple of days on, a gigantic schoolkids choir corralled in the studio. Chris conducted them. I think he'd been in a choir at his school, Prince Alfred College. Chris, from Keith, a South Oz township, a boarder at PAC from age five, he said. Small wonder he'd bolted with our band of gypsies.

'You are my children, but why are you killing me?' So went *Goodbye*, this Oedipal farewell to our blue planet going grey, already on the cards in the early Seventies, scientists warning of what they called the 'greenhouse effect.' The choir brought *Goodbye* to life, but David still not sated. 'I can hear things on it that aren't there,' he said. 'Well, good dope will do that,' said Mauri. 'No, I mean it needs more sounds.' Mauri's nonplussed. We all were. 'How do you mean, *more?*' Silly question.

'The whole thing?' said Joff. The studio today, full as the Pacific. 'Yeah,' said David. 'Just the one.' Those *more sounds*, the Sydney Symphony Orchestra. All of it. Over-used, that word genius. But not here. John Robinson from Blackfeather scored the charts and conducted the SSO that day. It was full-tilt unreal. From cutting singles on the fly to this, our own private *Sergeant Pepper*.

FORTY

The news, not good. Brisbane show, already blown out twice. We've just landed in the rain on the redeye. Two fetchits from the headliner's crew met Headband at the airport with some ace bud for us, arranged by Ray, self-invited along as 'roadie,' and Gene. Our accom, same as the stars of the show, Brisneyland's snazzy Parkroyal. *TF Much.*

A major get, this, on the bill for the Rolling Stones' first swing down here since '66. Down to Gene's stout powers of persuasion, Headband were already the hot contender, and an act of goodwill had sealed it. The Stones, shy a proper grand piano for the show, and no local hire house would cut loose a Steinway or Bluthner for a pack of rock'n' roll bangers. Then Gene thought of the white baby grand at the Whisky. Had it trucked up to Brizzy, quid pro quo the Stones convoy to cart it back down for the Sydney shows. So here we be.

But outside now, the end of days. *'Queensland sunshine super state,'* sang Chris, a tourist ad of the time. The rain, like roofing nails poured on corrugated iron, and he's trying to make us laugh, lift our spirits. No one dared say it. This tour, all outdoor shows. *What if they cancel the whole thing?*

For Headband, a late gig last night, then pre-dawn check-in at Sydney airport, so forget about bed. 'So best crash out now, reconvene later in the foyer,' I said.

An hour plods by. Sleep won't come. Then a rap at the door. A moment's ice in the belly. *I'm holding that bag of green.* But cops don't knock. So I swing the door open, pull the face into shape for a smile and a *no thanks* to housekeeping.

Oh. 'Hi, man. You Peter? I was told to come and see you.' I search for words. 'Come in,' I manage. *Just like I'd heard. Takes care of business, direct.* 'Bad news, I'm afraid, Peter,' says Mick. *Pe'ah.* 'It seems we're in danger of being hit by a cyclone. But we don't want to let down the fans.' *Let dahn the fans.* 'So we'll play a short set, a gesture, you know. Thank the brothers and sisters who came in spite of all this. But there's just one hassle,' he said. 'Our techs tell us it's well dangerous. Water and electricity, you see. Could lose our lives.' He spoke as if ordering from a menu. 'And the thing is, man, we don't have the insurance to cover you guys for that.' His face told me the rest. He paused, let it sink in. 'I mean, we really apologise. But would you mind awfully to just be our guests instead? Assuming we survive the show, we'll have a big party.' *Par'y.*

So then. Denied a go to take on *the greatest rock 'n' roll band in the world.* But an invite few ever get. *Party with Their Satanic Majesties.* I remembered that bag. 'Like a joint, Mick?' He grinned. 'Nah. Can't now, man. Things to do. Maybe after the gig.' Then we both saw it, the *Courier-Mail* on the table. Front page pics, Mick and Carly Simon, of his backup vocal turn on Carly's *You're So Vain*, a sidebar yarn to the lead story of the Brisbane blowouts. 'How was the sesh with Carly?' He shuddered. '*Ugh.* Those huge lips,' he said. I looked at his huge lips and let it go.

So I called 'em up. *Meet downstairs. Important.* Sailed down there to find it swamped. Road crew, band molls, journos and shooters, tour managers, all that mess, my three bandmates huddled on the perimeter. My news hit hard. But even as I spoke, a cosmic joke at our expense. Breaks in the gloom, the sun out again. 'Might clear up after all,' I said. Just as it vanished and the clouds burst afresh.

Here in all this teem, Jim Oram, a search and destroy Sydney journo with whom we'd become cobbers, on the chat with the Stones' press officer, Les Perrin, who they all called 'Lunchtime.' Gene and Ray in there somewhere, and *Go-Set* shooter Philip Morris. Other liggers, rockpigs, desperates various. Gene said let's make the soundcheck, watch how the Stones work. A roadie, beckoned by Ray as if our valet, drove us. To happy up, a fatty I'd skinned up from that little green bag, to spark up on the way.

Insane. Stage aswarm at Milton Tennis Courts. Fifty of them, the crew, give or take, slaving in the wet. Hardcore roadpigs. Our mob, in a circle under cover, sidestage, ripped to the skull. Stones crew on the goey or coke, to be sure. Their pilot here as well, big black pupils, a voice from far away. *Peaking.* Hit me with a Q. 'Hey, man. What country are we in?' Nicky Hopkins emerged, plonked himself down at the Whisky's baby grand. Plinked out a few notes, then pulled out a yo-yo. Basic throws, then tricks. Rock The Cradle, Around The World, Walking The Dog. Horn section Bobby Keyes and Jim Price soundchecked their mikes. *Parp. Beep. Rawk. Buddluddluddle.* The crew being bossed about now by this beefy unit, cracking the verbal stockwhip. Ian Stewart, head of road crew these days, booted from the Stones onstage lineup in those image-fixated early Sixties. But still played a mean Johnnie Johnson, Chuck B's genius piano banger.

We met Paul Dainty there too. You'd never pick him for a promoter. Talked soft, walked softer. Peter Rudge, the Stones' manager, apologised for bringing out the English weather with them. And we had a yak with some of the crew. To ignore them, just asking for savage retribution, a thousand ways to fuck our set sideways. Sydney still to come, so we schmoozed 'em good and thorough.

Back at the Parkroyal, we're bailed up by a music journo, the formidable author of *Lillian Roxon's Rock Encyclopaedia*. 'Whoever I sleep with tonight,' declaimed Big Lil, 'will wake up famous tomorrow,' as she eyed off Chris. He gave it a swerve.

'Hey, fellas!' *Whoa.* This one's masked, like a Batman villain. *Catwoman.* 'I'm Mrs Richards,' she says, meaning Keith's wife. 'How about we ride up to my room, do some smoke? I'll get Mick in to meet you all.' Good cause to hide the face, this unit, but we only learned the full bloodfreezing story later.

It wasn't exactly Motley Crue. Stoned, up in her suite, a craving befell us, so from room service, tea and biscuits it was. 'Mrs Richards' had the mask off now, to reveal a red target painted on her forehead. A lost verse from *Honky Tonk Women,* this one. Passed a jay and picked up the phone. 'Mick, darling,' she says, a voice all husk and gravel, 'come say hello to Headband.'

So I meet Mick twice in a day. Total charmball, again sorry we couldn't play, assured us we'd be loved up, full VIP, post-show. Meanwhile, 'Mrs Richards,' who Mick called 'Kathy', slipped into the bed, under the covers. And *now he crawled in with her.* Inexplicable at the time, but I think trying to convey to us that this whackjob was *not* Keef's wife. Then he leaps up, hadda lotta things to do, he'd see us later. *La'er.* We left soon after, still no clue that we'd been well and truly played by 'Mrs Richards.' Nor of the havoc to come.

A couple thousand hardies out on the grass in the rain. Out they stroll, none of the swagger you'd expect. 'It's gonna be a very short show,' said Mick, long scarves looped around him, cummerbunds draping at his sides. Shiny jacket. Pants, blue, embossed with silver stars. Across his forehead, a headband, a showgirl's plume poking up out of it. Most of all this he removed and flung aside, one item at a time, as they ploughed on. Leroy Leonard, Mick's twice life size bodyguard, scooped it all up and stashed it when not perched aft of Keith's armoury of open-tuned guitars, clapping along.

The show, a scatter of hits, some numbers off *Exile On Main Street,* their latest, buffeted about by wind and rain squalls. At one point Nicky stopped mid-song. Pulled out his yo-yo as Stu sauntered over and took his place. Then, over. Less than an hour. And quite terrible. Had we played, we'd have blown them into the Brisbane River.

Up in the Parkroyal's penthouse, hillsides of delectable eats, platoons of drink waiters circling. We gabble and chat to media liggers here, selling Headband hard. *You wait till Sydney, man.* Some time on, they made an entrance, almost in squadron formation. Keith, contrary to legend, most affable, didn't lob knives at us or anything. 'Hey,' I said, a bit bolshie by now, all that smoko and now just add liquor on board, 'I thought you guys were the greatest rock'n' roll band in the world.' Keith half-smiled. 'Yeah, well, man, we are.' But I'd seen otherwise. 'Well, I thought you were shithouse tonight.' Mick jumped in. 'Yeah, well, *Pe'ah,* as you saw for yourself, it was a shithouse situation. Well awful, man.'

Mick peeled off to work the room, but Keith gave all four of us one on one time. To me, to talk of his piano heroes, Johnnie Johnson and Jerry Lee. And Vytas Serelis had sold a painting to Mick Taylor, I learned. Swapping Vytas yarns with Mick T, I see Bill Wyman, statue still up the back of the room, away from the hum and boil, as if some mime artiste hired for this bash. A Stone of stone.

'Me?' I said. 'Ramsey Lewis Trio, Bobby Timmons.' This, to Charlie Watts, of NYC jazzers we both liked. Also, talk of players with whom I'd worked in England. Big or no, Charlie knew them all. Small planet.

The Stones, well, so normal, so *English.* Nothing of the Lucifer's goblins that their first manager had fashioned. And happy to share the fruits of their fortune. In Keith's book *Life,* he offers laudable recall of that tour, bar one place of which, not a syllable. *Brisbane.* That Bananaland bud maybe. Or Mrs Richards. The worst was yet to come.

FORTY-ONE

Oh fuck. En route to the airport for the flight back to Sydney, a semi on its side in the rain. And spilled from the tray, smashed to shards, the Whisky piano. *Abe Saffron's piano.* I wondered how Gene would get us off the hook. *The kind in freezers to hang sides of beef.*

'Hey, Gene. Can I snag some Stones tix off you?' The face he gives me. 'You off your trolley, Peter? These are rare as moonrat's piss. I can't just...' So I serve him further and better particulars. 'Well, see, Gene, it's Boo Boo. Her, er, *boyfriend* wants 'em.' The spliff drops from his gob and he goes pale as a snap-frozen ghost. Rummages in a drawer, flourishes a fan of them. 'Tell Mr S, my compliments.' He doesn't mention the piano. And no way I was game to.

'Give that mad judy a big miss.' Back at Chequers, Ray's word to the wise. Our pal Mrs Richards a world of botheration, he'd heard via tour security, bruisers from Bob Jones' karate dojos. The night before we'd flown into Brizzie, Mick J, who'd said a few things to the media of our First Peoples, had been invited to a Brisbane showcase of Indigenous art, dance, bush tucker, then was monstered by someone there in all-over black body makeup. 'Guess who?' says Ray. 'They had to bounce her out of there, biting and scratching all the way.' And this, not the last of it.

'Jump in, Headband.' Ray drives us there. A white limo he's hired, the size of Gracelands, and lays a jumbo joint apiece on us to scarf up on the way. Boo Boo's along for the ride. A police escort the last part of the way there, at the lights and straight through the crowd at the racecourse.

We're all hyped up over what we'd cooked up last night. 'Fuckin' ripper,' said Ray when we told him.

But first, *this*. Royal Randwick, fifty thousand in the afternoon sun, wired on this or that, bound for off the planet. Different piano onstage. *Don't ask, Peter.* We didn't rate a soundcheck, so had no notion what we'd sound like. We opened up, first chords, first number. Ga-BOOM. *Was this ME? US? The volume.* The crew had left the soundboard set on full turbo roar, giving us all they gave *them*. We howled through our set, surfing barrels of rolling thunder, punters flattened and thus compelled.

Time now for our surprise. Ray and Greg Rosman set down a white canvas sack centre stage. We dropped into *Children's Dreams*, our nine-minute opus. The moshers down the front noticed first. *That bag. Moving.* Hands emerged, waving about. Arms, ditto, bit by bit, all of Boo Boo, in naught but skin and beads, save sliver of silver bikini. Boo shimmied into a feral bellydance, the horde delirious now. She spun and bolted from the stage to tsunami of whistles, howls and whoops.

Follow that, Mick. We played on, white hot, boiling over. Then the signal from the Stones crew sidestage. We cleared off. Quick.

'Come on in, yo.' Leroy Leonard at their dressing room door. They're warming up, *Love In Vain*, other bits of other songs, as Leroy serves drinks. A dude he calls The Doctor happens along, black bag and all. That's when Leroy has Headband step outside 'for just a few ticks, you dig.' From behind the now closed door, cackling laughs, *oh yeahs*. Someone's getting zoomed up good and liking it a lot. Then the door swings open, a couple of crew emerge. *They're gone.*

'Look! Over there!' It rocked towards the stage, from the far side of the course, little white lights all over it. The sound, rising as it neared, hooves at the gallop along the straight. White stagecoach, six horses to match, the Stones within. Had to hand it to 'em. *Game over.*

They ripped it up as the sun went down, stuff off *Sticky Fingers, Exile On Main Street, Let It Bleed*, two Chuck Berries. Wound up with *Jumpin' Jack Flash* and *Street Fighting Man*.

'Here! Toss these fuckers into the crowd!' All too soon, show's done. Their road crew, thrusting buckets full of red rose petals at us and our plus ones, Mouse, Wendy, Janne, Pandora, as the crowd goes full frenzy. I'd say forty crew, management, blow-ins like us, all flinging the stuff at the mob. Others pitched buckets of ping pong balls, a rain of red and white. Above us, fireworks. Big finish.

'So you really are the greatest rock 'n' roll band in the world,' I said backstage.

'Yeah,' said Keith. Smile all teeth this time, in five shades of brownstone, gums of dull blue. 'We know.'

After-party at the Hyatt Kingsgate, a bacchanalian blowout, and next day we did it all again. Midway through the Stones set, we spy from sidestage a couple, in silver body paint, worming through the bobbing mob to front of stage. She's astride his shoulders, he in a Roman gladiator costume, hers a Cleopatra headdress. Mick's dropped into his karate dance moves, these two doing them in sync. He spots them, turkey-struts over. Cleo extends her hand for a kiss, he takes it, and she yanks him forward, plants a sloppy on his moosh. The Stones, still pumping full bore as Mick shuffles backwards over to Keith, hand mic behind his back. 'That fucking Cleopatra. It's Mrs fucking Richards!'

That tour, all too short and too much fun. A shame, what came next.

FORTY-TWO

'But our earn was three grand.'

'That piano, Peter.' So vibed up after the tour, it was some weeks before I flashed that we'd not been paid. About to say *not my problem*, then I see Gene's eyes, gone to ice. We didn't play the Whisky for some time either. A further penalty, perhaps. Best not dwell. Nor press it.

Back on the plough now, Chequers, the Mandarin, Stagecoach. And the Manzil Room. The *Mandrax Room* most called it, after that pill cooked up to shut down rowdy psych patients, now a first call party drug. Yep, the Mandy, where all the Cross went when all else had closed. The contents, hookers, junkies, bogans on bucks nights, hoons, outlaw bikies. Grifters and crims. Doormen, borderline psycho. And the odd OD on the premises or close by. One time, lugging out in the alley in the pre-dawn murk, Greg and Tooley came a gutser when they tripped over a corpse.

'We don't call the cops, mate.' And it wasn't just the Mandy. This enforcer at Stagecoach clocked our faces when he came upon us one night, out in the lane for a joint. His burden, a firey's carry, over the shoulder. Dropped it like a sack of blood and bone mix. 'We *are* the fuckin' cops.' The EMI studio, now our only refuge.

'We're just walking past, and we hear *this*. Had to find out what it is.' Americans. Older dudes. The elder of the two, familiar but couldn't place him. We're in the control room, sonic cosmonaut Mauri on the other side of the glass, in a booth, a fiddle bow to his Les Paul strings. The elder gent sussed my confusion. 'I'm Benny Goodman,' he said, smiling. 'And this is Joe Pass.' *Spinout*. The Benny G All Stars Sextet, touring Oz at the time. To meet Major Jazz Gods, well, chance won't pass this way again. So I called a break, never mind the clock ticking away all those dollars. A special day.

'Well, that's fourteen hours I'll never get back.' This day, David had Joff in there, re-tuning his drums from twelve of the moon to two in the arv. 'To the same key as each track,' his decree. A touch of megalomania or maybe OCD issues, Fookesy, but always raring to go when we lobbed as the Town Hall clock chimed at midnight.

It was Headband's Altamont. Charity fundraiser out wild west way, Oran Park Speedway, Campbelltown. 'Can't buy this kind of promo,' said Gene, explaining why we'd been dropped into it. This turn, for Foundation 41, medical research for disabled kids. Big bill. Sherbet, Ted Mulry, Jeff St John, Pirana, Spectrum. Sundry others.

And guess who else. A swarm of sharpies shoved their way to the front, laid siege to the stage. Started up that stomping thing, in time to us, so we stopped playing, to chop it off at the socks. Wrong move. These numbskulls, the floor all theirs now, went at it even harder and louder. Joff, full steam pissed off, chucked his sticks at these lamebrains, up to their buzzcut rat's tails mullets in cheap booze and rough speed as a full-on brawl erupted. We cut it short, shot through. Fast. For the Gospel Of Headband, no converts to be had here.

The Sutherland Shire had little taste for us either, nor the others on the bill that day, Pirana and Lotus. Out in the Shire they dug Sherbet, Ted Mulry, Skyhooks, and we weren't any of them. At the Taren Point Youth Centre Dance, Headband no match for an all-in punchfest.

'Thank fuck for the Sav.' It was our get outta Sydney jail card, as close as it got to a weekend retreat. Three hours north of the crazed of the Cross, the Shire, the Wild West, lay the Savoy, an ex-Hoyts in Newcastle turned over to live music. Red velvet stage curtains, chandeliers, rounded art deco corners. The gig, an all-nighter. Headband doubling with Sherbet and Ted Mulry Gang, two such that come to mind.

Newie, mad for Joff, his sombrero, his hairpiece trick. And went berko the night he bowled up during Ted Mulry's set and sang *Jump In My Car*. Beyond bizarre, and they loved it well.

Close by Chequers, a shabby shadow of its once were, lay the Mandarin Club. Manager Denis Wong had started up Chequers with brother Keith back in the 50s, then later in '65, opened the doors of the Mandarin, a mere stumble away. Wily move. The 'Chow Club,' badged thus by the offhand racism of the day, stayed open till dawn, for the crowd spilling out of Chequers at two or three AM and up for more. Crims loved it, they too open all night, and so, ideal for transacting business. Then in '65, the Wongs opened the Whisky and Stagecoach. Saffron, far as we could tell, owned most of the Wong Kingdom now. Denis managed some of it still, but only the Mandarin to his name alone. Yet held his head high.

'Chinese as they come, Peter,' said Gene. 'Loves a haggle. He was offered the Beatles once. He says *how many in group? Four*, they say. *OK*, says Denis. *I pay for two. Bring two out here.*' Monday, payday, I'd collect from Gene, then drop in on Denis. 'Ah, Peter. Always on time. Very good. *Jolly* good,' chuckling. The English language, to Denis, a laugh riot. Envelope, always correct weight, handed over with a bow at the neck. Not like most, their dead eyes and frigid silence when parted from cash.

'You Australian *knobheads!*' Here he was. With Thorpie in tow. Keith Moon, out on the ran tan, in Sydney for a stage show of *Tommy*. A few days back in Melbourne, at the after-party at Molly Meldrum's, he'd hijacked an unattended public transport bus, the driver off having a leak or something. Molly, with Jim Keays and Doug Parkinson crammed into his Mini-Minor in weaving pursuit, managed to board the bus when Moony stalled it, and wrench him out of there before the cops got wind. But tonight, he's *our* problem. To follow up his how do, Moony lobs a full can of KB Lager at us. Had Ray not known who he was, Moony would have flown home in a bucket.

The other band played a set now. Pirana, might have been, or Country Radio. Billy and Keith, tripping, eyes black and a-glitter, but keeping it together, veteran riders on the LSD Special. Moony quite chatty, as if the other had never happened. 'Just his way of saying g'day,' said Thorpie. 'Not to worry.'

And then Moony wants to get up for a blow. The punters go berserk when Chris calls him up, but, well. He's way out of time with us. *Rank,* our facemakes to each other as we wade through a blues. And he cut his hands on the cymbals, bled all over Joff's kit. Ours not to reason why. On with the show.

Country Lady released now, our maiden Polydor single, a teaser for the sooncome album. Burned to the top of the charts in Adelaide, a good part of the way there in Melbourne, even teetered at Number Seven for a time in Sydney. Headband were *in da house.*

A second go on *GTK* when they let our new long player out of the gate. Playing live as per, but this time just one song, the album's title track and new single, *Song For Tooley.* A Joff lead vocal, not Chris, true to our pledge that every song on this disc differ from its sibs. And a strange choice for a 45, *Tooley,* a prog aria with complex changes. Of local artists that year, apart from the usual power ballads, MOR evermores and plagues of teenage TV dollies, airplay was given over to straight, no chaser blues and rock'n'roll. *Tooley's* flame flickered barely a week, soon blown out by that howling gale of Ozboogie, of Thorpie, Band Of Light, the La De Das and all, not to mention Helen Reddy, Jamie Redfern, Sherbet and such. Headband, not so much ahead of its time as in a parallel universe, circling some Einsteinian warp billions of light years out past the Milky Way.

At the time the *Tooley* album hit the stores, Gough Whitlam had just bought Jackson Pollock's *Blue Poles,* and the Queen was out here to open the unfinished Sydney Opera House. Our LP shifted just two thousand units across eight weeks. And then sold no more. The deal with Polydor, well. Gene didn't need to tell us.

Headband were booked now on a lot of bills with the Ted Mulry Gang, joints like the APIA Soccer Club at Leichhardt, and a big fandango on a barge in Sydney Harbour for 2SM. 'Get some fresh eyes on you,' said Gene. TMG not mega yet, but close enough to reach out and touch it.

There was another reason for doubling with Ted and his Gang. Their bass player Steve Hart had bailed mid-gig. Ted scooped up the bass Steve had flung down on the stage and boxed right on. Next day, Ted asked Chris B to fill in for now. Then a few weeks on, asked Chris to join TMG. He knocked them back. Staunch. The way the wheel was spinning for us by now, I'm not sure I would have.

FORTY-THREE

In the last days of '73, we glanced up to see buzzards making circles, crows massing on the power lines. Record deal kaput, album dead in the water. Ahead, naught but slogathons in soundcaves dim and skanky. Going by record sales, no one knew who we were. Come to that, nor did we, Mauri the first to say it. A sonic soup, ours, of all styles under the moon. Lost at sea with no direction home. Wherever *that* was.

And other torments now. Gene moved us from Chequers to the Whisky. The run, eleven weeks, six nights per. Not so bad. All the free hooch and boof a body could hold. But your one night off, sacred. That's when Whisky manager Denis Wong decided that the band he had playing on that seventh night, our night off, was redundant. *You men I pay top money*. Our obligation, the way the big D saw it, to also work that seventh. *Not need other men. All men sound same. No problem.*

Joff blew all the gaskets he had at Denis. So we didn't work that seventh night. Nor the other six any longer after Denis called Gene about it, and all save me found that they no longer cared. Burnout swept our ranks like typhus. Then Tooley bailed from our burning airship. Sydney, wound up way too fast for this gentle soul, pining for the old home town.

'Peter. Can I talk to you and Mauri alone?' Hamish was in town, on his way home from England, his gruesome duty there to lay out Fraternity's corpse. 'They want to resurrect Frats back home. Mick Jurd, John Bisset, not starters. Just Bon, Bruce, John Freeman and Uncle. So.' Held his hands out, *whaddyasay?* 'Ultimate supergroup.'

It had its merits. *Working with Bon.* But bouncing Joff and Chris, just not on. We four worked together too well. And Frats, a rolling tavern brawl even at the best of times.

Then about a week on, Fate spread its cards on the barrelhead. 'Soldiers brave and true,' said Chris. 'No easy way to say it. But I'm out. I'm sacking myself.' A better offer, he said. *'Solid Air',* we're calling it. Like the John Martyn song.' This, a new rock show, to be produced out of ABC TV Adelaide, Chris tapped to be presenter. I said the only thing I could. 'You'd be nuts not to.'

Hamish already knew when I called. News rips around Adelaide fast as herpes. And he had a new venture up and humming now, he said. Wooden toys, building kids' adventure playgrounds. Peppertown, he badged it. Getting out of our game. Me, wondering what took him so long.

We packed our way better halves and rugrats back home. Band itself couldn't just cut and run. Obligations. A week in Melbourne, booked months back, and two in Perth. To skip out on old mate Saffron, unwise.

Greg Rosman didn't jump on that last chopper out of our Saigon. Work to be had in Sydney for good road crew, gazoodles of it, and Headband's last ride only for the damned, he decided.

'Melbourne, sure. The rest, forget it.' Ken Booth, roadie supreme for Perth rockers Bakery, signed up for our last go-round there.

'Rooted. But I know this bloke...' Out between Thomastown and Coburg that morning, Big Red went *kablam*. We piled into Joff's car and snailed it through hours of traffic snarl and Ken's directions out to Sunshine or somewhere. There, this auto boneyard, a new low in chop shops. Night falling, Ken fitted a new engine block jacked from fuck knows where, and brought the Red back to life. Nothing to lose now, for our last swing round Melbourne we played whatever we pleased. And those infamous deadface crowds loved it well.

On to Adelaide, a catchup with close ones, and hired on roadie Dave Colvill there for the trek across the Nullarbor. A creature of wonder, Dave. Skinned a champion spliff, a Grand Master at packing cones. Cooked hot breakfasts, drove Big Red like to make the old gal fly. As a soundo, well, we should have had the smarts to record what he whipped up on the board. *Headband Live!* A coulda shoulda Great Lost Album.

After the Perth expedition, we'd agreed, fade to black. Hamish, other ideas. 'Go out with a bang,' he said. Headband's mighty *espirit de corps*, cracked and brittle now. But, yeah, they said, they were up for it. One condition.

'No more than this,' I told Hamish. 'Two in Whyalla, for Mauri. And just two in Adelaide, the Bridgeway and the Findon.' I had my reasons. 'Don't want to jeopardise the finale.' Our farewell show I teed up myself, February 1974. The big room, Festival Theatre.

The Eyre Highway hell of the Nulla now. Then the Perth scene, jumping hot, but scanty glimpses all we saw between shows, a frenzied fortnight, booked as full as Gene could make it. Then, home, foot to the floor. I forget who said it. 'Can't be late for our own funeral.'

First, the last stand on Mauri's home ground. They loved him, our rough boy from the Alla, afire on all eight. Stamped and whistled for more. Our Mr Berg could do no wrong. The Bridgie and Fiesta Villa, Headband honed to hero class now, from those blood on sand arenas of Sydney. Gave 'em all we had. They knew it was the last of us and roared accolade.

'Sold right out,' said Hamish, every seat at Festi Theatre. Adelaide had never lost faith. We played nothing but *Tooley* that night, our one and only album, stem to stern. They knew all the words, these two thousand believers, and sang along with every song. Headband went out like fireworks at midnight.

FORTY-FOUR

I blame Suzi Quatro and *Devil Gate Drive*. I asked them round to our pad in Frewville to lay my brainwave on them. 'Well, Pedro,' said Mauri. 'A miss is what I think I'll give it.' Joff, same. 'I didn't know Robyn played bass,' he said. She didn't. *Never in my life, Peter,* when I asked. But played a little guitar, so surely, too easy to make the switch. *Voila,* Robyn Archer, Headband's new Chris Bailey. Yeah, nah, *you're outta your skull, man.* Not that they said so. The looks on their faces enough.

Quite right, too, I fast came to see. We'd have crashed on takeoff, no Bailey on board. But to snuff out that Headband fire, a high crime. So, then. Maybe a new name, new songs, my fresh ruminations now. Rope in Robyn, Joff, Mauri. But not only them. Bon Scott maybe, other Frats. And jazzpals from the early times. Then it hit me. Why small town bands die young. A dozen gigs in, every head in town has seen the show. So what if *every show is different?*

I knew over a hundred singers and players. *A lot of us write, too,* I mused to the moon by the glow of a bifter. OK then. Originals only. But a three chord limit on them. So that anyone could play them off a skim 'n' scan rehearsal.

I called this newborn after a nickname for a mob of us who used to go sweeping the slopes for gold tops in the mists of the uplands, the higher peaks east of the Adelaide Hills. And so was begat the Mount Lofty Rangers.

'Country rock. Three chords, no waiting,' I said to the crew I asked round. Mauri, Vince, Philby Colson, relocated from Sydney, Vytas, Joff. Bon, Bruce Howe and John Freeman from Frats. And more. Way more.

The first blow, a big garage at someone's pad, I forget whose, out in the burbs. It was *fun*. A doz of us that day, loud, loose and dirty. *Funkolossal,* Philby's take on it. No sonic wall too thick or high, Bon's voice slicing right through.

We worked up a songbook, contributions from all among us who had readymade numbers in their swags, forty-one all up, and so named the charts therefrom the *Mount Lofty Rangers Top 41,* with Vytas Serelis cover art. And we lured players from quarters other than ours. Trev Warner, fiddle and mandolin, a great get. At times, first violin from the Adelaide Symphony, Brian Porter, well up for some improv, the air of a joyful escapee about him. An accordionist rocked up one day, that sound from under the bridges of Paris. *Yes!* Took me a while to notice. *I'm enjoying this again.* Bon not the Rangers' only singer. Often, he and Robyn Archer in tandem. Those two made sublime harmonies. Stars fell on us every show.

'Peter. Alan Slater here.' Chris Bailey a Rangers regular too. Having a bash at going solo now, Chris, off his TV profile from *Solid Air*. My brief at Slater's this day, produce a single, the theme from the just released *Sunday Too Far Away.* Star of the film, Jack Thompson, had cut a version, but RCA had signed Chris and thought it might chart in the hands of a rocker.

So I pulled in Phil Cunneen, guitar and bass. Myself, electric piano and a Solina string ensemble keyboard. State of the art, this gizmo, and Slater's had one. Local jazzer Dean Birbeck, drums, and for a pinch of alt-country a la The Dingoes, Uncle John Eyers from Frats dropped in a dollop of harmonica. I wrote two key changes in, to pep it up for radio. Mike Fitzhenry, a brilliant engineer, flew the board.

Not a hit. No clue why. Then *Solid Air* was axed. Of his solo stab, Chris reported that he 'did two gigs and was paid for one of them,' in between slavejobs as dishpig and landscape gardener. Such be the life.

A pillar of the Rangers, Chris, for its first years. Played with us when Bruce Howe or Phil Cunneen couldn't. Then said *I'll take it* to an offer to spirit him out of there. That year of '77, going places off their single *Am I Ever Gonna See Your Face Again,* Angels singer Doc Neeson released himself from playing the bass, to be freed up for feral stagecraft. Doc and the Brewster brothers, John and Rick, had been part of the rock 'n' roll patio furniture round Adelaide for yonks, with Moonshine Jug And String Band and the Keystone Angels.

I had to smile when I heard the Angels' first hits. See, I'd taught Rick that Chuck Berry voodoo back when Rick first took up an electric. He'd only ever played acoustic in their jug band. Useless for the Keystones, a rock 'n' roll outfit, strumming an electric like a folkie. Those tips, the base of *Comin' Down, Take A Long Line, Marseilles.* Rick stood frozen onstage playing that and the world threw its gold at them.

Yeah, well. Wish I'd thought of it.

FORTY-FIVE

'So, Peter. A bit of a pickle.' Robyn Archer, trying out for the New Opera of South Australia's debut show, *Threepenny Opera*. Needs help. Me, puzzled. She'd done Brecht-Weill before, at loads of gigs, and had played Annie One in *Seven Deadly Sins* at Festi Theatre. 'Well, chum,' she said, 'they require that you sight-read music. So I told 'em I do.' She chuckled down the phone. 'Thing is, I don't.'

Alright then.

We met at the Lion, its piano down in the tunnels. Went through the sheets they'd sent, where the notes were on the keyboard, then the stave notation. Robyn looked like she was grasping it. Didn't tell me that she memorised as we went, by ear. *Not by sight.*

Come the day, Robyn stepped up, stuck the dots on the stand with that easy flourish of the schooled. Then proceeded to *pretend* to read it, aped me in mime. Faked it. Did she get the job? Take a wild guess. Before too long, a major exponent of Brecht-Weill worldwide. So goes the brave Archer. No sea too wide, no star too far.

It was round about now that Ron T had Robyn and I back in the tunnels there, our solo turns. And on other nights, the Rangers. Bon sang every show we did down there, with Robyn now and then, or Joey Moore from the kids' shows on Nine. Philby, Chris Bailey or Phil Cunneen, Mauri, Joff. Banjo players, violinists, local jazzers for saxes and trumpets. Some days, up to ten of us, a thing of epic dimensions.

One day, Bon and I set up the band outside the pub, on the footpath, corner Melbourne and Jerningham Streets. Pulled three tons of passing trade. Illegal as hell, yet no noise from the blue meanies. Ron T just walked on by, kacking his big head off. Had the Higher Powers well looked after, to be sure.

Those Rangers Lion gigs, never dull. It was a Friday night when this house painter barrelled in, grogged up, primed to punch on. Doormen bounced him and most would take the hint.

'Fuck's *this?*' Bon, Philby, faces splashed with something. 'It's *metho!*' From an air vent at street level above the stage, the nutbag aforementioned, with a water pistol full of wino's choice straight from his ute. Philby and Bon herbed up there and grabbed him. The bouncers sat on him till the cops arrived. 'Cheap bastard,' said Bon. 'He might have squirted us with Jack D.'

Once, we played the Old Lion Disco, midnight to dawn. 'All yours, Biggles, after we punt the mugs.' Here, space for a thousand heads, and we filled it right up. Well, Bon did, loved like a newborn all over town. Mouse cooked eggs and baked beans for all this horde of stoners famished. *And they never stopped rockin', till the moon went down.*

Carey Gully, the Acres of Vytas, the place to be Sundays. Pubs shut tight, the only place to get a drink, Adelaide's charmless airport bar. Up at the Gully, Vytas and others jammed on sitars. Bon sang. Bassplayers Bruce or Chris, drummers John Freeman or Joff, stringbusters galore. Mauri, Philby, others. Apart from Bon, singers from Robyn to Stephen Foster to Sue Barker to Vince Lovegrove.

Vince brought Jack Thompson up there once, Jack in town doing post-pro for *Sunday Too Far Away*, to blow some harp. A tasty player. Another day, Garry Macdonald, riding high on ABC TV with the *Norman Gunston Show*, in town for a part as a cop in *Picnic At Hanging Rock* and no slouch on the blues harp either. Those Gully blows, some of the wildmost shows the Rangers played.

'The way I like it, Peter.' With Bon as a Ranger, we played all over, all the time. The Lion. Flinders Uni refectory, Barr-Smith Lawns at Adelaide Uni, or Union Hall, for students. Or all night stirs at Carclew, with Schmoe And Co, Sue Barker And The Onions, scores of others.

And somewhere in the swirl of all that, a muse from beyond the heavens bestowed upon me a vision, of a whole new stage where Bon could shine. The first spark of *Lofty* came to me off that Aussie thing. Redheads called *Blue,* or tall people *Shorty.* Bon, all dash, perfect as James B. Lofty, bushranger and highwayman. The Rangers Top 41 as soundtrack, ideal for what I had in mind. Much of the Rangers' repertoire spoke of bushrangers, moonshiners, tableaux from our colonial past.

'A musical, you reckon,' said Bon when I laid it on him. 'Sounds like a blast.' *Lofty* still just a seed in my mind awaiting sunlight and water. No storyline yet, but a notion of one, based on the Kelly Gang and their practice of chucking parties for the towns they held hostage when they robbed the local banks. They were outlawed by government decree, or *wolf's heads* as such were called in mediaeval times. Anyone with a shooter could drop 'em where they stood, no Qs asked, and bag the reward, the bounty on their heads.

'Lives bound to be short, so might as well be merry,' I said.
'Yeah,' he said. 'That sounds like me.'

Yep. Without a word of a lie, Bon had a taste for musicals. Sang the hell out of showstoppers from *West Side Story* or *Porgy And Bess* when the mood took him. But we never did get to work together on our planned collaboration. No one saw Fate, masked, pistols drawn, hiding in the bush by our highway of hopes and dreams.

FORTY-SIX

'You play some guitar, right?' Philby calling. 'Your students will show up, have no fear.' Well, I like teaching, and it paid alright. Among Philby's pupils at Yatala, Chris Worrall, the Truro murderer. Pre-Milat, pre-Snowtown, Australia's worst serial killer.

Weird at first, sitting down with a convict, the screw posted sentry outside the door on the snooze as often as not. This program, a bid to stave off riots like the boilovers at Bathurst Gaol that year, these now all the talk in every tank from Darwin to Grafton to Hobart.

We weren't to go off-road with the cons, they said. No talk of what they were in for. Guitars and how to play them, nothing but. But we looked more like the crims than we did the warders. They soon let us know they knew what we did for fun. More than some of them, in for dealing. Busted with a single plant even, you'd be in the frame as a grower, and they'd drop hard time on you. But that ain't no crime. Way I saw it, a public service. We owed these fellas a favour.

BB King Live At Cook County Jail, *Johnny Cash at San Quentin* or *At Folsom Prison*. A fad for a time, live albums from the big house. At Yatala on Sundays, they put on church choirs, plays, folk singers. So I told the superintendent that a Rangers show might move more inmates to take up guitar. An easy sell. Anything to stop the joint being burned and razed.

Bon, mad keen. 'Did some juvie at Riverbank back in Freo.' Philby, Mauri Berg for guitars. Chris Bailey, bass. Fiddler, Trev Warner. Joff Bateman, drums. Janne Berg and Lo Furler, backing vox. Myself, electric piano. Screws wouldn't come at the Hammond.

'No way, fella. You could cram a ton of smack into that bugger. Or shooters.'

The set, a scorcher. The cons, nutso for it. Show over, as they're locked up for the night, the bush telegraph in there came alive as we were leaving. Clapping. Whistles and hoots. We couldn't see them but knew somehow they were on their feet. For this was a standing ovation.

'*Hey Bon!*' From up on those tiers. '*Thanks for coming!*' from elsewhere. '*Yeah! You're a legend, Bon!*'

And he was. And is.

'Yes. But we're still friends.' Vytas, of Lo Furler's forbearance now exhausted. She called time on their union, the law to dissolve it. And with Lo a free agent, well. Movement at the station.

'I've got the hots for Lo, Peter.' Well, few didn't, but Philby chose to act on it. Stationed himself one arvo at a bus stop where Lo got off on her way home from work, teaching now at the Art School.

'G'day, Philby. How would you be?' A voice at his back.

'Oh. Hey, Bon. What are you doing here?'

'Well, you see, it's Lo. She gets off here, and I've got the hots for her.' This as the bus pulls up and Lo happens on the scene.

'Oh, hello, boys. Sorry, can't stop. Got an appointment down the road here.' Had them sussed. That look they get on, like dogs. Philby and Lo did end up together, for some years. Had a daughter. Sia. *That* Sia.

'What the fuck? You stink!'

'Wallaroo Fertilisers.' Bon's bike at the kerb, the moon on high. 'Got two songs here, Peter. Can I have a shower and something to eat?'

Chucked in his last job, he said, scraping barnacles off the hulls of ships. 'This one pays better. Dawn starts, down the Port.' Shovelling shit, blood and bone into sacks, then hefting them on to trucks. These lyrics, coined in his head as he slaved. 'Wrote 'em down at smoke-oh.' He cleaned up while Mouse cooked him a feed. I got on the piano and we banged those words into melodies. Goofweed and Jack Black to nudge the deal along.

End product, *Clarissa*, a ballad of a Bon ex, and a tear it up rocker, *Been Up In The Hills Too Long*. Both went straight into the Rangers' songbook.

I'd wondered what it might be like to live in that Futuro flying saucer house in Slater's car park. And came to find out right about now when things pretty much broke down between Mouse and I. The upshot, best we live apart, and relocating Mouse and the kids not a feasible option.

Way it went, Vince Lovegrove had vacated the Futuro in recent time, and so I asked Alan Slater if I could bunk down there while I scoped around for something more permanent. My first night in there, drowning in all that self-pity and desolation that fate rains down on the failed and fallen of wedlock, Bon came looking for me to offer solace, bearing a bottle of Jack and some ripper homegrown. And a proposition he laid on me.

'You gotta be able to fuck to it.' He meant something suggestive, a touch of erotica.

'Sure. Anything else?'

'A bit of humour, you know, naughty but nice, not too serious.'

'Righteo. Got a key in mind?'

'Well, it's for a single, so I wanna hit the top notes of my range.'

'No worries. What might they be?'

'Oh, fair go, maestro,' this chuckled through a cloud of smoke. 'You might as well ask this joint here.'

I had a keyboard in the Futuro, so I fired it up and played snatches from some blues and such in a mess of keys as Bon sang along, testing his range. Turned out he could hit a high B, a note well beyond the reach of some trained singers and most of the rest. The deal here, a big one as these things go. Bon had decided he wanted to track a solo single.

'I really dug those 45s you did with Headband, you know.' He meant *Land Of Supercars* and *Country Lady*. He was after a number from that sonic locality, 'that'll pull a few ears at the record co, you know, give 'em a stiffy straight up.'

Bon, still with the reconstituted Fraternity at that time, but they'd continued to slop scorn on his stabs at songwriting. 'Toilet poetry, they reckon,' so just as he had at Frewville a few weeks back, he chose to chuck in his lot with me.

'Too much. Far out, yeah, just like I pictured it,' he said. 'It's a smash!' I stayed up all night writing *Round And Round,* knocked out a solo demo at the piano. Bon swung by next day for an earful. He liked to work hard, like me, and fast, likewise. So we dropped it straight into the Rangers' set, test-ran it at the next couple of gigs.

The Futuro was a crash pad deluxe for a head with naught but the scant earn that gigs brought in. Two levels and just the one of me. A sumptuous black leather couch installed on the upper floor and in the dome of the ceiling up there, huge hi-fi speakers so that the music shone down and bathed you in its goodness. Mouse and I kept it cordial despite our estrangement. I even had little Lo over to stay the night. She loved it, didn't want to go home. 'It's like a spaceship, dad.'

Meanwhile, back in Bonland, round two weeks on, we were ready.
'How much you got on you, Bon?'
'I dunno, twenty notes,' he said, fishing it out of these high-waisted flared jeans that he alone could rock, worn like a bushranger would have.
'Same here,' I said. That day, we pooled our forty dollars to book the two hours of studio time it would buy us at Slater's.
I corralled Lo Furler and Janne Berg to double up on the backing vocals to save time, and because they sounded ace together. Brought in Chris Bailey for bass, Randy Bulpin guitar, Lee Cass, drums. A crack crew to nail it fast.
'Summertime, and the livin' is easy...' Setting up a mic sound at Slater's, Bon rips into *this*. He'd now and then make with a line or two of Gershwin, or Scottish folk classics. *'In soft purple hue, the highland hills we view...'* Once at a Rangers soundcheck, a burst of Gilbert and Sullivan. Knew it all. And so few knew.
'Ah, again, if you would,' I said from behind the glass. Randy's trying to lay down a solo, spooked by the little roughnut with the possum's eyes. Bon's necking Johnnie Red from the bottle, getting *that look* on, his night sky stare. 'Nah, not good enough,' his appraisal after every pass.

Me, used to it, but if you didn't know Bon bar his rep as a scrapper... Randy landed a pearler two takes on.

'Does the bizzo every time, Peter,' said Bon through a chuckle. 'Calls up the wild thing.'

Round And Round utilised the full band and backup vox, and so ate up the lion's of our time, but thirty minutes remained still when the stardust settled on that one, so we tracked *Carey Gully,* a ballad from the Rangers' set that I'd written with Lo Furler in mind to sing it. Just Bon and self, his two vocal tracks, lead and harmony, both bullseyes in single takes. Me, piano to back Bon and then I dropped in some guitar.

'I really hope this happens for you, Peter. Hope it works out.' Bon to a tee at day's end, wishing me fortune bonny. Nothing came of it until years later, no way in Adelaide back then to bag a record deal, and we two, not much clout at the time with the industry Godheads Of The East, so it was a quest soon abandoned. But Bon all the way in my book, not about what was in it for him. Not ever.

There'll never be another.

FORTY-SEVEN

'Here, give this a burl, Peter. Guaranteed to blow your mind.' It was at a Rangers rehearsal down in the Lion tunnels. Had I known how Bon had come by this hash from far Lebanon, I might have been less impressed.

Home from the Frats shipwreck, Irene had called game over on their marriage, made her own way back into the world and rented her own place. With zero life skills, Bon's homeless, crashing at Bruce Howe's down at Semaphore, in denial. Couldn't leave Irene be, round there on his Suzi 500 pretty much daily, into her for handouts. And this day, a blazing bridge too far. She's not home. The rent, in a jar. He knew where. Next day, she let him have it. Banished, evermore.

'He dropped the bike out in the street last night. Pissed as. I took him to task, riding round on that fuckin' rice burner with a skinful.' Rangers practice again today, Bruce on the steam and whistle, and Bon an hour late. Not like him, for all his wild dog ways. 'He's herbin' all over town, off his dot...' This, even as Bon fronts, all reek of strong drink and rage. 'What sort of a time you call this?' says Bruce. Bon's ratshit, bottle in fist, murder in his eyes. Myself, Mauri, Philby, Joff, know that snapping and barking at Bon only looses the wildcat, and freeze. 'You're the dickhead got us where we are today!' he shoots back, not up at all for a Bruce *bad dog* routine. So Mauri and I try another tac, *easy, tiger, we'll give you a lift home*. But it's a bottle too late for that. Bon's eyes, *gone black*. 'Fuck you!' at Bruce. Swerves to the rest of us. 'Fuck you all!' Wheels for the door, smacks into the wall. Takes two more goes before he gets through. We hear the Suzi chug into life. And the bottle. *Smash*.

Nelson's Wine Bar, South Road, too small for the Rangers full ensemble, but Nelson, Portuguese, tall, hard and salty like some caravel skipper from the fifteenth century, always up for trios and quartets made up from our number. John Freeman's trio on that night when Bon comes in swaying. 'Hey! How about I have a sing?' *Oh, fuck no.* John, no bulldog Bruce, but can't cop him in that state. 'Bon, forget it. Keys.' *Gimme.* But he's past reason, livid at John's ixnay. Nelson, a generous host to all of us. Food, wine, mull. A tussle in a roomful of his punters, just not on. John let Bon go when he barrelled out.

'He's in the ICU. No visitors. In a coma.' Irene calling, three AM, from the Queen Elizabeth. 'Cactus.' I knew before she said it. 'Might not make it to morning, Peter.'

Three days in that grey zone between life and the other, then he came round. Before me now, in smithereens. Gashes across his throat. Wired jaw, cracked skull, ribs. Big picture, a Frankenstein work in progress gone wrong. Tubes in mouth and nose, drip fluids into wrist via cannula. Neck brace, bandages, plaster holding together the remainder. 'Well, the tatts are still there, so there's that,' he croaked through a grin shy its front teeth. Saucy with the nurses, asking would he ever be well enough to root for Australia again. Pleading for more soap *there* at bed bath time. 'I think it's still dirty, nurse.' Most would wear a slap in the moosh, full deserved. But he had them Bonstruck. And us. In time, all the world.

But for now, he'd smashed through the windscreen of a moving FC Holden at near terminal velocity and would need months to mend. So for the time being, *Lofty* a no go. But we'd all still be there for him when he came good. How could we not be?

'Just between you and me, Peter, this is for Irene,' said Vince. He had work on offer, for me and our convalescing friend. Some weeks on, Bon's out of the QEH, no home to go to. So Vince and wife Helen had him at theirs, with Bon's mum Isa flown over from Perth for assist with the nursing. In time, on his feet, walking wounded. But tapped out, so he's round at Irene's again, putting the bite on. She called Vince, all tears and grinding teeth. 'So, then,' said Vince, 'you see that he does the jobs, and I'll drop some cash on him. Give Irene a bloody break.'

And Vince not the only one. Alex Innocenti hired Bon to staff his boutique a few days a week. Maybe Vince had put the arm on Alex, I don't know. Anyway, I dropped by one day, and there's Bon, all tan suit, fat paisley tie, flared pants, lapels wide as Moon River. My guess, the one he was married in. Bon's being there made the shop a cool hang, and that must have sparked a few sales. Or a wave of shoplifting, although all hellfire awaited any who tried to filch from Alex. That cat could see round corners.

'Look out for cops, Peter,' said Vince. Only time for it, 'tween midnight and first grey of dawn. No-one about, even the blue trouble thin on the ground. This poster run, for a Sydney band Vince was touring. Had a thing on the radio, *Can I Sit Next To You, Girl?* A glam feel, all Alvin Stardust, Gary Glitter, T Rex. But a gutsy edge, like Slade.

'Singer's not up to much,' said Bon. I held a king size sheet against a wall. From the bucket we'd mixed, he slopped flour and water glue over it with a yard broom on a sawn-off handle. 'Should be these dills doing this for us, Peter.' He winced at some pain or other. Still limping, in no shape really for even light yakka like this. Made what came to pass even more amazing.

'Ninety notes. How's that for value?' Bon's bought a shitcart Holden, a powderblue Belmont bomb. Not even roadworthy, but things in that regard slack as back there, back then. Vince had also engaged Bon as a driver, to ferry touring bands around. This crew from Sydney, on the grumble. Their singer a real stone in their shoes, the vibe from the little toughies in the back seat.

'Take it from me, George.' Vince, on the phone. 'Bon is your boy.' It was PhoneHead who got the logs rolling. I'm at the office, taking poster art to the printers. 'Is George the George I think it is?' I ask. 'The same,' said

Vince. The boss Easybeat, now mentor to sibs Malcolm and Angus. 'No go on anything without his imprimatur.'

'Nah, I don't think so, Vince. They're just a gimmick band.' All Bon had seen of them was the promo pics. That kid. Schoolie cap, shorts, schoolbag. The rest, glitter, satin, platform boots. Not Bon's go at all. Then he saw them play.

'They're a kack!' We're out on a poster run two nights on. He flashed a smile, new teeth in place of those lost in the prang. 'PhoneHead dragged me out to the Bridgeway. Those guitar players, too much. Singer's a bignoter and a sook, just like they said, so we pulled the brothers aside, told 'em their troubles are over. They looked me over and called me an old cunt. I said I can outrock you to billyo and back. They said *fuckin' prove it.*' He chucked me a devil's grin. 'It's on for a blow tonight.'

Bruce Howe, wife Anne and their little one had moved from beachside Semaphore to Prospect, north-east of North Adelaide. Sometime round midnight after ACDC's gig, Vince brought over Bon, Malcolm and Angus. The new Frats there, having a blow down in the cellar, their rehearsal go-to these days. High talk of a giant PA they were building, but no gigs to speak of, and in no rush to get the circus on the road. No wonder Bon had climbed aboard the Rangers. Bruce bass, John Freeman, drums. Mauri Berg, who'd joined Frats by now, out in the shed, building speaker cabinets for this monster rig of theirs. Uncle on deck down in the hole too, for some boogie chillen on the harps. They say it went all night.

"He's gone, Peter,' said Vince. I'm calling around, lining up a Rangers gig, three weeks on. The Seedies had swung back into town. Singer Dave Evans had been punted by now, roadie Dennis Laughlin filling in. Bon had jumped up for a sing at the Bridgie, said Vince, then did three nights with them at the Pier. 'Shot through the morning after.'

I pictured it. A small travel bag. Stash of skins and dacca, spare Levis, t-shirts. Possessions beyond those, forsaken where they lay. Travelling light. And fast.

FORTY-EIGHT

'We'll make a pilot. To sell them a series.' It was halfway through '74. Henry Prokop, a producer at ABC TV. His brainwave. For *The Mount Lofty Rangers Show*, we'd be paid, but no more than union, to keep it low budget, 'to convince the hand-wringers that this puppy's doable.' It meant access to tech crews, editing suites, recording studios, all of Aunty's magic caves. And it would screen all over Australia, flinging open doors for the Rangers to the venues of the nation.

The pilot ep, two halves. First, a live show at Adelaide's ABC studios in Collinswood. Robyn Archer singing up fire and rain, Philby and Mauri, Chris Bailey, Trev Warner and Brian Porter, Rick Kent on the drums, Uncle's harmonicas. The rest, location shoot, Carey Gully. Here, all the Rangers who could be herded, dancing about, pulling faces, lugging a flagpole about and planting it, hoisting the Rangers flag, a Vytas creation. This, for the *Mount Lofty Rangers Theme Song*, tracked at the ABC.

It went to air soon as we'd wrapped, still warm. Viewers must have been elsewhere that night. Aunty's verdict, swift and harsh. The ABC's crews better occupied covering lawn bowls, chess news and Royal visits, the judgment of the killswitch gorgons.

'Can you sling me a gig, Peter? I'm skint.' Vince brought him round to mine. He'd joined an outfit in the UK called Esperanto Rock Orchestra, 'a twelve-piece ticket to hell,' he said. 'One way.' Glenn Shorrock split from Esperanto and made for home when he could abide it no longer. Glenn and I had bumped up against each other across aeons, my bands on bills round Adelaide with his Checkmates, then the Twilights, later

Axiom. The Twilights and Axiom had troubled the charts again and again, but Glenn here today had the cast about him of a fella hammered flat, beyond consolation. 'Yeah, made a lot of other people rich,' said Vince. 'Haven't we all.' Vince tossed a bag on the table and reefed out some skins. 'Got a tape here you might want to bend an ear to, Peter,' he said. 'Some songs Glenn here wrote.' Some killer stuff there, titles like *Statue Of Liberty, Meanwhile*. 'So,' I said to Glenn, 'Can you start Monday?'

Robyn the business upfront, but Glenn, a real bonus, a bona fide rock star coming on board the good ship Rangers with a swag of monster songs. Yeah, hits they'd one day be, but we did 'em first, at a new gig I'd hustled. Now, Robyn and Glenn our frontpeoples, betimes Vince Lovegrove or Joey Moore, at Festi Theatre Amphitheatre. Outdoors, in the round, playing to the summer Sunday masses out on riverside Elder Park. Mick Jurd on guitar, ex-Frats, now back in town. Some days Philby, Mauri and Chris B, of course, or Phil Cunneen, with Joff or Rick Kent, drums. Randy Bulpin a few times. A magic tableau.

'Well, I can't say no to that,' he said. And fair enough. Glenn didn't stay a Ranger long. Joined in around November '74, then come December Glenn Wheatley called. 'The deal is we work up the act, based in Melbourne, then next stop USA. No fuckin' about,' said Glenn. He was moving on up the line, with Beeb Birtles from Zoot and Adelaide stayer Graham Goble. Mississippi they badged it, American market in mind. Then changed it. Something more Australian, they decided, yet would pass as international, off a sign on the Princes Highway en route to a gig in Geelong. Little River.

FORTY-NINE

'*Cocks off! Cocks off! Cocks off!*' It was March 1975. North of here, the fall of Saigon. Meantime, a rabble yowling for our gizzards at the International Womens' Day gala, Festi Theatre. Robyn Archer on the bill and keen to sing some jazz, had me assemble a band. 'Best in town, Peter.' So Freddy Payne, trumpet, Geoff Kluke bass, Dean Birbeck drums, Grahame Conlon, guitar. We both said it at once. 'Can't go wrong.'

'*Cocks off! Cocks OFF!*' But just not on for the Separatists, as they were known then. Robyn tried to reason. *These are feminist men, ladies. Here to help our cause.* Result, the Seps exploded. Climbing over seats. Making for the stage. *For us.* We took it on the toe, down into the dressing rooms, locked ourselves in. A riot up there now, two thousand strong, set to search and destroy. The theatre manager, seized and dragged up to the gods, dangled upside down. It fell to the ushers to persuade them to unhand their hostage. No cops called. Would have made things far, far worse. The gig, well, show's over, folks. We didn't dare surface till they'd run dry of rage and dispersed.

Days of loathing and mayhem followed all that year. The endgame, Whitlam sacked by a drunk in a top hat, then cast into the outer darkness by seething voters, garnished by ugly near-riots wherever Whitlam's usurper Fraser showed his face at rallies. Flipside, SA Labor, by no less than a miracle wrought by Don Dunstan, his the sole surviving ALP regime now save Tasmania, and Don keen on boosting trade with Asia. Via Dunstan's ministers, Penang in Malaysia, our sister city, invited the Rangers to be part of a cultural exchange program. For this run, Trev Warner, Chris Bailey, Rick Kent, Mick Jurd. Dave Colvill, roadie deluxe from the Last Days Of Headband, fulfilled that same for the Rangers only tour.

We played ten nights in Penang. My song *Adelaide* served as our de facto promo jingle. Along with that, we included Bon's *Clarissa* and *Been Up In The Hills*. Others by my hand, *Carey Gully, Round And Round, Mary J*.

The hangman's noose for ganja here, so we packed no smoko. No need. Kids on the streets, bulk Buddha sticks for sale to *mat selleh*, Western tourists. Hotel rooms only for mull-ups, *Do Not Disturb* slung over locked door. Gig o'clock, we're genial and charming envoys, smiles that wouldn't quit spread across our faces. Herb superb reaps diplomatic triumph.

'Of course, I'd love to,' I said. A gun songwriter, by the dawn of '76, Robyn Archer had amassed a good hand of goers for a solo album, and dragooned me now to pilot the musical director's wheelhouse. We tracked at Slater's. Self-funded, no label. Where the dosharoonie came from, as ever with Fort Archer, the talent not saying. Tight budget, so a pile of pre-pro, to avoid blowing exy studio time. To the Lion tunnels and its piano we went, daytimes empty of punters, to write up charts for feels of far pasts, of Prohibition speakeasies, bierkellars of the Weimar Republic, of old-time English music hall.

From the vast ranks of the Rangers for the sesh, Nic Lyon, multi-wondered, violin, viola, acoustic bass. Russ Johnson, guitar and bass, or jazz and country maestro Grahame Conlon. One song, a Dixieland feel, so sometime Rangers from Schmoe and Co, Schmoe on clarinet here, Freddy Payne's trumpet, Geoff Kluke, bass. From the Rangers Penang Six, Rick Kent's drums.

Robyn's songs, well. *Menstruation Blues, Dicks Don't Grow On Trees, The Old Soft Screw, Neurotica Suburbia*. Soundtrack to the wildest movie never made. *Take Your Partners For The Ladies' Choice*, Robyn's first long player, wasn't released for another year. Indie records, from farm to turntable, a slow train. In the pressing plant queue, aft of the majors with their million sellers. No matter. A mighty body of work here.

Roy Rene had created Mo McCackie, Australia's W.C. Fields, our Buster Keaton, our Chaplin. *Young Mo* was a new play of Roy's early years, his South Australian backstory, by Steve J Spears at The Space, Festi Theatre. Steve calling now. 'Our piano player won't come at a bush tour.'

The *bush tour.* Everywhere and more with anyone still in it. Fifty to a hundred heads most nights. And the vibe in those little town halls, peace in the valley and high on the hills. No liquored-up grogans or sharpies, no psycho bouncers, no blue cadavers in the lane. I didn't know how to deal with it.

Cast of six for *Mo,* Robyn dominating as vaudeville legend Queenie Paul. Me, there to back the song and dance routines for *Let Me Call You Sweetheart, A Nightingale Sang In Berkley Square,* the chartbusters of Mo's times.

'A musical? Bon Scott?' I'd cast aside all hopes and dreams of *Lofty* when Bon left town with ACDC. Then for some reason mentioned it one night to Rob George, the actor playing Mo, and a playwright. 'Tell me more,' he said. I explained that I had those Rangers songs fit for purpose, the slim ghost of an idea based on the bailups of Australia's craziest bushrangers. 'Oh, Peter,' he said. 'I see a hit right there.'

'Not much to do in a country town,' said Rob. 'A South Australian one, less.' In our down time he and I set to now and developed the 'book', the script. Snuck into halls before shows or hung around after curtain at the piano, and here brought *Lofty* to life.

There was no way Bon was a starter for what Rob and I conjured up. The Seedies, out on never-ending tours now of anyplace that would have them, George Young a true believer in a thousand gigs maketh the band. Didn't faze Rob. He'd fallen in love with our creation. He and *Young*

Mo director Malcolm Blaylock had put the arm on for an arts grant to stage it, and bagged us ten grand. And so here we be, auditions for *Lofty* now. I'm at the piano at Union Hall, at an hour aforenoon and foreign to me.

'Looks just like Bon,' said Rob. 'Only taller.'

'Yeah. You could say that.' Twice his height. Wayne Anthoney did have Bon's cheeky twinkle about him. Sang alright too. For Lofty's gang, we cast Tony Strachan from *Young Mo*, Michael White likewise, and John Francis. Joey Moore aced it that day, a smokin' *Me And Bobby McGee*. Just had to be Lofty's offsider, saucy Black Alice. As Lofty's Smokin' Sisters, Wendy Wewege as Crumpet, Sue Wylie, Gail Castanetto. And Maureen Sherlock, a face well known from TV work.

The Bushrangers, Lofty's band, Rob left to me. Mauri Berg, Phil Cunneen, gun drummer Mark Meyer, self at the 88s. But as per Rangers custom, guests every show. Trev Warner or Brian Porter, or Graham Davidge, his flute and guitar, and Davvo's ways to make 'em talk and laugh and sing.

James B. Lofty, a mashup of Mad Dog Morgan, Ned Kelly, Captain Thunderbolt. Black Alice, based on Mary Ann Bugg, First Nations companion to the bold Captain T. The story, well. Lofty and the Smokin' Sisters, minstrels at Queen Adelaide's wedding, are transported to the colonies for singing bawdy ballads, 'Queen Adelaide' being a cheap Riesling popular at the time.

Lofty escapes custody. He and gang take townships hostage, knock over their banks. At post-heist parties, Lofty, his band and the Smokin' Sisters make up the floorshow. The plot, yes, flimsy as they come, based on those birdbrained Elvis clambake hot rod Hawaii-sur-Vegas flicks of the Sixties, but action abrim, a chassis to hang songs on. The venue, Her Majesty's, born 1913 as the Tivoli, for vaudeville and musical comedy. Perfect.

Sets for Lofty by Vytas, in Vytascope. Lofty and his mob die en masse in the final shootout, as heroes must, the blood price of liberty, then rise in bushranger afterlife paradise, their eternal reward for having stuck it to The Man, Lofty ascending via the grinning beak of a towering model flaming galah Vytas built and painted.

The whole, a Bon Scott might have been, my unrealised vision a soundtrack album *tour-de-force* for Bon's monster talent, and a new star on the musical stage. Such are dreams, fireballs roaring by, fading all too soon, leaving only that silent midnight blue.

'Well, why don't you rob the pub?' It was Ron T's brainwave. The *Lofty* run, about to open. Ticket sales, sluggish. So we rounded up fifty heads, garbed up as bushrangers and assorted ne'er do wells, plus the cast in costume and character. Tipped off the media and made offerings to the gods for a slow news day.

A horde of Rangers thundered up Melbourne Street that Sunday in APCs, jeeps, old bangers Vytas had resurrected up at Carey Gully, and some on horseback. We barrelled into the pub, *Lofty's* cast going large for the news crews. We liberated slabs of beer, bottles of Scotch, and roared off in a convoy of mayhem.

It was all over the TV news that night, the papers next day. Result, *Lofty's* first five nights sold out. And Ron's pub, choked with drinkers, diners and disco dancers for weeks after.

Crafty bastard.

We opened January 28, 1977. '*Lofty is big on fun, but a bit short on being the country rock epic it boasts.*' The only critic there, Ian Meikle from *The Advertiser*, less than enraptured. We'd billed it as 'an epic tale from the annals of country rock' as a joke, a pisstake on those gushing blurbs that come with every refried retread of stale old Broadway classics. We made it through eleven shows before they closed us down, five shy of the season booked.

There'd be no second run, and no *Lofty* for Melbourne or Sydney. And no soundtrack album. Now if Bon had been on board…

I think half of Adelaide rocked up, as per when word gets round of a good one. And at the end of run party for *Lofty* that night, two big names were playing at different venues across town. 'Eh, Peter!' I couldn't believe it. Round midnight, Bon's rocked up at Jo's. Bottle of Chateau Tanunda brandy in hand, one more inside him, by the looks. He clocked Jo's eyes on his tattoos. 'I can show you *all* my tatts if you like,' he says. No sale. Nor Rob George's wife Maureen to his *how about a root?* I think he passed out not long after that. Maybe just as well. Jo told me later that this other singer, also playing in town that night, had got wind of the shindig. But the joint so packed, I didn't even see Rod Stewart on the pond.

'Your ticket's at the box office, Peter. Make sure you come see me before the show.' This, a couple of nights on, the last of a three night stand here on their *Dirty Deeds* tour.

'Yeah, a Monday night, y'know, and *Adelaide*,' said Bon, pouring Jack and Cokes backstage. The Apollo held near three thou. Tonight, third of three, full house. Many overseas acts couldn't match it.

'Angus, this is Peter, the guy I told you about.' I'd expected them to be surly, insular, but we had a great chat about that Sydney scene of the early 70s. Me, a terrible musical snob, not into this blitzkrieg brand, but bags of regard for what Angus wrought from that SG of his. And told him so.

I was down the front with the hordes who'd swarmed there from the first chord, Angus astride a roadie now, a move he'd go on to do with Bon as his steed. They forded into the crowd, Angus blazing on the SG. As they swept by, he shook his head like a dog after a swim. Me, deluged in sweat. A full immersion ACDC baptism.

I'd not see Bon for two years after that, such did their fame grow. I was happy for him. We all were. Survived a pot bust, the world's worst grunt jobs, beatings, the doomed quests of others, and cheated death on a dark highway. His karmic reward now, all he'd ever wanted, that which had eluded him for so long.

'Never sick a day in my life, Peter,' he said when we caught up two summers on. 'Any bugs get in me, I grab a bottle of neck oil and *bam!*'

FIFTY

We kept the *Lofty* lineup of the Rangers going for a 'Bushrangers Ball' up at Flinders Uni, on a bill with the Bogaduck Bush Band. Then assorted players through '76, the first of '77.

Robyn Archer busied beyond time for us now, and Chris B bailed and jumped on The Angels express somewhere in there. It was a great break for Chris and full deserved, but he never grew accustomed to being an Angel. 'Fuck, I miss Headband,' he'd say whenever we caught up down the line. 'That lost oasis of our serenity. This mob, at each other any chance they get. Medic!'

So now, of we Rangers, Jo Moore, Vince Lovegrove and Steve Foster upfront. When they were free, three I dubbed The Smokin' Sisters, like their namesakes from *Lofty*. Marlene Richards I'd worked with in those faraway days of the Mac Men. Sue Barker had her own blues outfit, the Onions. And from Sydney, new here, dominating around the new fad of piano bars, Sybil Graham. A folkie mate of Steve's, Les Wahlqvist, also sang here and there. As did Jamie Swann, earthshaking voice, pipes of an operatic baritone. Now and then, from way back whence, Irene Petrie, and Barrie McAskill, The Bear, king of the hill in our town back in the Sixties, home now after a long time gone in Sydney town.

And Vince told us of this kid he'd seen. The next Bon Scott, he said. 'I'll get him along to do his thing.' Well, Vince made the show but forgot to bring the kid. It never came to be. The Rangers Top 41, as only Jimmy Barnes could slay 'em.

But everything you love dies. The Rangers' prospects, dwindled now, venues favouring the young lions of a new pub rock boom. The last Rangers show, back at Yatala. No Bon or Chris B this time, but they dug it full well. A fitting end, dispensing cheer to friends in need.

So where to now, Peter?

All over town now, these New York-style piano bars. Acts to match. Triple threats, cats who could sing as well as play and get on the yak with patrons, stand-up schtick. My one out of three didn't cut it. But cash at ebb tide and two kids still at home bid me set forth to make a new me.

At the piano and solo, Sybil Graham worked a room like nothing I'd ever laid ears on. Slayed 'em with funny stories, and invited requests. *And knew every single one they pitched up.*

'I always work alone, Peter. Only way to fly, darling. No-one to depend upon but yourself.'

To me, a new continent found. Sure, I'd worked solo, but never engaged with punters, just a tinkler in the corner. 'And I never tour,' said Syb. 'That way lies madness. Let the world come to *you*.'

Right on, Sybil. A picture I could dive right into. Just one hassle. I'd never been asked to, or perhaps not allowed, and I'd never pushed it. On our home planet Muso, custom decreed a hands-free singer up front, or the player with the best vocal chops. And me, serene as the shine of the moon that I didn't have to front the show.

'But you've been singing for a while, Peter.' It was Mouse who reminded me. With the Rangers, I'd sung my songs to Bon, Robyn, Glenn Shorrock, to show them the melody. 'You sound like Randy Newman,' said Bon one day. 'Nothing wrong with that.'

And Syb told stories, yarns of the songs' creators. So I, too, love it or loathe, would have to *speak to the punters,* find within me a brand new bag. And to awaken that sack of tricks within, a guru.

'I'm just down the road from you.' Sybil bid me drop by at hers when I took to catching her gigs to watch her read and work a room. 'Daytime is playtime,' Syb's credo. Liked the wine and the smoko, but ten thumbs at assembly. 'Did time with some Jamaicans in London,' I explained as she watched me roll up a whopper.

'Clive! How would you be?' He was doing yearly tours of Oz now. A laugh with Georgie Fame at Syb's over our face-off in London ten years back. At Sybil's, between her tutelage in the ways of the piano bar, a rolling party, off Syb's years in Sydney and for a time as pianist for Barry Humphries. Georgie one day, another, Carmen McCrae, out from the US. Tales of Billie Holiday, Louis Armstrong, Ellington. Or the sultan of Sydney clubland, Ricky May, in town for a show. Now and then, a jam. The neighbours, serenaded by the best of our times and never knew.

'Peter, darling. You free?' Syb pulled two to three gigs *a night*. Some, thrice-weekly, or both the lunch and dinner sesh at restaurants. One place, Chateau Fort, its basement now a bar created just for Syb, their sole act. I'd been slaving over a hot piano for months, but now, I'm ready to rip. Tried out my new show on Syb one day round at hers. Next I knew, I'm doing jobs she can't make.

Oh, and one other thing. They'd got it wrong forever. *Beagley* as *Bagley, Beasley, Brearley, Bailey*. Once, wait for it, *Beastly*. Even real names spelled right, well. *Elton John* stayed with you. *Reg Dwight* didn't. It came to me in a flash, this name of a town in Scotland and a 'burb down near the Port.

'Even Australians can't fuck up the spelling', I said to Mouse. So I snapped it in two and made it mine. Arise, ye varlet, Peter Head.

Now some of these piano bars soon morphed into all night long clubs. Like Jules on Hindley Street, run by George Polites, son of property gigabaron Con. Revolving signs bearing his name, *Polites,* atop his buildings, lest we forget who owned this town.

Jules, a local take on Studio 54, that NYC hang of the stars. And like 54, Jules featured a celeb guest list, ridiculous dress regs, a velvet rope and barred to all but those granted *entre* by the style enforcers on the door. Yet jammed to the gills, any night of the seven. A disco with DJ up to midnight. Other side of that, me at the keys 'til three.

Across Hindley, a short roll down from there, a joint they called the City Hotel. In reality, a front bar with a piano, the City being part of a proper big pub, the Mediterranean. The Med had big room out back, Countdown they called it, for the big touring acts. The piano bar here ran six nights a week, Syb and self at the *de rigeur* white baby grand. Syb from 'round midnight. Me, three AM to six, darkest hour to first light.

My favourite.

The City opened at twelve of the moon, knock-off time for hospo toilers, bar staff, chefs, waitpersons. Across the witching hours after that, in would roll the sex workers, drag queens, crims in all shades of the shifty.

The rub 'n' tug reliefers and the trans crew, the friendliest of this mix. They'd request songs and shout me exotic drinks. Slow Screws, Harvey Wallbangers, Fluffy Ducks, Grasshoppers, Brandy Alexanders, White Russians. A perk that would one day prove costly.

Bands on tour oozed into the City after their gigs out the back. Partied hard as diamonds. Still going as the world outside woke to their stale hell beyond this funhouse of the moontribes.

'Can you tell us your name?' I was able to recall *Peter Beagley,* still on my driver's licence, and who the PM was. In a coma, I'd been. 'Out for twenty-four hours,' said the nurses. Driving home at dawn, my blue Kombi, T-boned hard and fast, stage left. Hit and run. Yet I'm still breathing, nothing broken. Mine, luck rare and special, denied most.

'I was never here,' he said. My *thanks* was a croak, all I could summon. The ambos had come on the scene before the cops. One of the paramedics, now bedside at the RAH. 'Found this in the wreck,' he said. Passed across the bag of dope and went on his way with a wink.

And there was something else those cops never knew, thanks to those angels of St John whisking me away. My sorry life, saved despite being blotto at the wheel. The Kombi totalled, so I bought a third-hand Holden wagon in Adelaide two-tone of white and rust, all blue smoke and rattles.

Karma meanwhile biding its time, all the patience of the First Nations.

FIFTY-ONE

At home, now Hart Street, North Adelaide, little Lo in primary, Josh at high school. As whipsmart as I'd been for a time, Josh, destined for uni, a place I'd only ever known as a cool gig to play. Our place, close to the old art school drinker, the Kentish Arms. One Saturday way past noon, gulping down a wake-up coffee, I see a crowd massing outside the pub. Might be a gig on. *Might be an in here.*

Got my head round the door to a surprise. There, the SA premier, Don Dunstan. Trademark white safari suit that only he could rock, all elegant cool, making a speech. A birthday bash. I sidled up the back for a listen.

I'd met Don D for the first time a few weeks back, the occasion his own 50th, at the Lion. He'd hired the tunnels. Private party, dozen or so close ones, Don at the other end of the piano, listening with *intent*. I felt honoured, being a fan of his brand of politics.

Now, speech done, he saw me up the back. Came over, grabbed my hand. 'Peter. I loved your playing at my party,' he said. 'I want to ask if you could teach me to play the blues. Like you do.' Played classical all his life, he said, but itched for a bash at the devil's. Then this. 'Would you like to come to dinner? I'll cook a meal, then we can muck around on my piano at home.'

Well, then. He wrote his address on a card. No messing about. Started that same evening.

'I won't be eating with you tonight,' was how Mouse and the kids heard it. 'A prior engagement,' I said.

A what?

'With the Premier.'

A Steiny. Full size grand, at Don's pad. *Play me.* 'You're a red man, Peter, I assume.' The wine chortled as it swirled into the glass. The Clare and Barossa Valleys, surely a lost chunk of the Promised Land.

'I'll show you what I mean,' said Don. 'What I've played all my life.' He rolled out an impassioned Chopin nocturne. By ear, no clangers. *Don has chops.* 'But what I've wanted to have a shot at, for years, was blues, jazz.'

He gestured for me to slide onto the bench beside him. I showed him a C7 chord, left hand. Then a C blues scale with my right.

'You can play any of those in any order. Sounds funky every time,' I said. Played them again, then he had a peck at it. Soon, he's banging away and *having fun doing it.* Every teacher's golden moment.

I showed him a few more tricks. He was rapt. *And something else.* Giving me little hugs and looking at me, well, sort of *funny.* Don, famous, to the haters infamous, for being bi. No big deal to me. You get practiced, working in showbiz, at how to let them down gently.

'I hope you don't think I'm gay,' I heard myself say. 'I'm sorry.' His face stayed in character. In his eyes, a wavelet of dismay. 'I am *bent* in *every way,'* I said. 'Except *that.*'

'No, no,' he smiled. 'Sorry if I gave that impression. I'm just excited about the music.' Then this, out of the blue. 'How about if I get some people around for a bit of a party?'

So. I'm at Don's table with the Prem, the Minister for the Arts, Len Amadio, and the Attorney General, Peter Duncan, talking of prevailing political problems. Len asked about the Rangers. It was clear he knew the scene well, his ear to the wind and the ground. *Well, it's the Arts Minister,* I thought, *pitch for some maybe one day funding.* I still burned a candle to the Rangers rising again. Len's intrigued when I explain the setup, its resemblance to a rep theatre company.

Then I talked to Peter Duncan, of dopers being jailed, people I'd taught guitar. Otherwise law-abiding, my arg, being minor pot growers their only crime. Yet alcohol, legal and sold hard amid its forever floods of domestic violence, road toll, sexual assaults, murders. He took it well. And penalties less harsh did come later. Our cab-sav driven convo, I like to think, one tiny seed planted to that end.

Don never asked for more lessons, but no wonder. Hard graft, keeping a progressive ship afloat in a town as Tory as they make 'em.

Down the line, they'd near kill him before they were done.

FIFTY-TWO

They were in town for just two shows, matinee and evening. Joe Pass, guitar, with the Zeus of my jazz Olympus, Oscar Peterson. Sold out. Mine, usual gig at Arts Festi time, the pop up piano bar at Festival Theatre, to lure showgoers to drinks pre or post.

Arvo shift done, I'm back on after a break as punters mill in the foyer for the Joe and Oscar night train. Corner of my eye, someone making for me. And timed his approach to match the last bars of *Moanin'*. This cat knew his jazz.

'Hello there,' he says. 'Didn't I meet you in Sydney? At EMI. Your band.' It's *Joe Pass*. Took me a sec to collect myself.

'Oh, yeah,' I said. With Benny Goodman. The *Tooley* sessions. I'm on my feet without thinking. Respect. He jerked his head, up there, upstairs.

'Coming to the show?'

'I'd love to, Joe,' I said. 'Bit short of cash.' The look on his face. *He's been there.*

'No problem. Come with me.'

My set, good as done. *Hell yes.*

Down we went to the dressing room behind the stage. There he was. 'Oscar, this is Peter. Piana player from the bar.' Joe explained my *fix*, he called it. Oscar grinning, *uh huh, uh huh*. 'Kid's got style.'

'Piano player, huh? Well, brother, I believe we can oblige you.' He gestured. 'Come sit over my side.' Oscar, at an eighteen-foot Steinway. No chairs about. So I sat on the floor, almost under that beast. Joe, other end, stage left. Best seat in the house.

An hour in, entranced, dipping into my jacket. A glance at Oscar. *Would he mind?* Nah, can't see it. And a joint is a terrible thing to waste. The smoke drifted out from under the piano, started to explore the room, drifting out into the audience. But no ushers pounced. None could see me so well-hid beneath that monster Steiny.

Then it was over. They rose, stood centre stage, took their bows. Turning to exit, Oscar fetched me a grin. And *winked*. Into the wings they rolled, to roaring, cascading acclaim.

Me, in floating reverie, almost forgot. *Oh fuck*. Made the bar just as the punters came piling in. Played like Oscar, a creature now of his divine muse.

The show's name said it all. *A Star Is Torn*. Director Rodney Fisher, also co-writer of the spiels for these legends which the bold Archer would inhabit. The range, vast. Needed two pianists, myself and Robert Gavin, a classical specialist. 'Rob for the *straight* stuff,' said Robyn. Me, down the other end. Where the wild things are.

Rehearsals, every day, several weeks, ten AM to four. Bare space, Festi Theatre, a Yamaha grand in it. Don't know how it went for Robert, but my half, one word. *Intense*.

Making charts in Robyn's keys, some differed to the originals, or were subject to changes as we went along. And all the while, Rodney critiqued Robyn's stagecraft, suggested tweaks, had us do multiple passes at each part of every song. Gave notes, like directors with actors.

'To be them, know them.' Some days, we didn't rehearse even, but back-and-forthed it in conversation, of those reincarnated here. Backgrounds, abuses endured. Deaths violent, sudden or alone. Robyn knew them well, but Rodney blew us right off the deck. His insight, like he'd known these people.

Ten days in, we're calling them Janis, Bessie, Judy, Billie, Patsy. As if our siblings.

Robyn's master stroke, a showstopper. For the whole turn, never once left the stage. Turned her back, mere seconds, or dropped down behind the piano. Here, bangles, beads, cowgirl hat, cocktail dress, gardenias, feathered headdress, at easy reach. From Billie to Judy to Patsy to Janis. *Snap.* Just like that.

And Robyn soundshifting. An uncanny thing, from Billie's soft, smoky purr to Patsy's twang, a voice *changing colour* as each new star turned to the footlights.

'She's so easy to work with,' said Rodney one day, Robyn out of the room. 'Not just punctual. Early. Smile that stays on all day. No tantrums.' He's unused to this, Rodney's a world of flighty thesps.

'Showbiz family,' I said. 'Cliff and Mary, her mum and dad, both in the game, and theirs too, back to her great grandma.'

'Part of her life from birth.'

'Yeah. Old school stagers. They bred a beauty.'

'Between them, almost thirty husbands. Two never married. Two were raped. And two were raised in brothels.' Robyn's spoken intro to *Star* had me all chills and fever, even in rehearsal. I'd have been happy as a seaful of clams to rock up to these forever, the joy it brought. But the tour under way now. I was on the bus for Canberra, then Hobart. Robyn was taking *Star* to Melbourne first, but not me. Paul Grabowsky lived there, a saving for a show on a skintight budget.

Truth of it, I was a little down about it. Way it rolls. And so, for now, back to the piano bars of a hundred moons.

'Peter.' Robyn calling. 'Bit of a snag here.'

'How do you mean?'

From the plane's window that night, Melbourne had never blazed brighter. Awkward next day, Paul bailing from the rehearsal as I rolled in, a nod our only exchange. I didn't ask. A mighty player, Paul, so the wherefore of his leaving the show a cold case for evermore.

'Whoa, Peter! We've got this gig *down!*' Robyn, stoked. Our show, *hot*, extended again and again. Five sold-out weeks at the Universal Theatre, a refurbished flicks palace on Victoria Street, Fitzroy. *Star* the first show to shake its thing at the old gal's resurrection.

I stayed in Brunswick, a stroll away from the gig. As the days rolled on, minor celeb status bestowed on me, recognised on Sydney Road, at the shops and so on. And a special traveller from Adelaide, for a time. Lo, now nine, on school holidays, stayed with me. Made the show every night. Insisted, then fell aslumber under the piano.

'Robyn?'

'Yes, dear heart?' We're in Robyn's dressing room. She'd taken great shine to Lo.

'I can do your show. Would you like to see it?' We were agog. Songs, spoken outros, all down pat. The showbiz bug within, stirred and arisen, preparing to fly.

'Um, Robyn, I should tell you.'

'Tell me what, Peter?' Out all night, me, with a pal from the Headband daze.

'Um, I dropped it last night. Still tripping.' Robyn said nothing, did the show. I found, or at least it seemed, that I played okay. Flashing still but on the low road coming down.

'Fuck, Peter.' *Oh, shit.* Called to the star's dressing room afterhand, I braced for a cold blade lining up the back of my neck. 'That's the best show you've ever played!' Said with a smile, not the first time one or both of us had played drunk or otherwise chemicalised. And we'd both dealt with Bon, his rolls and spinouts. But acid can take you to places you don't want to go. Labyrinths, with rocks rolled across, blocking the exits, and red eyes not your own in the murk. Best not go there again.

Canberra, June. Cold as an East River corpse. *Star* at the Canberra Theatre's Playhouse. Four nights. Brit comic Chris Langham, big as Russia then, on TV and movies like *Life Of Brian*, working the big room here. Came and saw our turn, befriended us right off.

And other diversions. We played Senator Susan Ryan's party at Parliament House, the old place, after *Star* one night. The new one, still a hole in the ground on Capital Hill then. Quite a bash, this, a celebration for women in politics, their numbers in parliament still far short of what they should be, but growing all the time. The actor Robyn Nevin, a terrific master of ceremonies that night. And Senator Susan, I presume, unattached at the time. Hope so. Chased me around all night. Flattering, but just not on. Couldn't help thinking, *what would Bon do?*

Perish the thought.

Hobart's Theatre Royal, 'a venue since 1837', locals told us. 'And *haunted*,' as all old playhouses are. Five nights, full houses. But at run's end, airport farewells with no talk of further. Nor the wild ride waiting round the bend.

FIFTY-THREE

'Peter, you been to the Territory?' Not *Star*, this job. Far, far from it. Funded by a grant. Ms Archer's coterie, grandmasters at gaming these dispensers of pennies from heaven.

In Darwin, we picked up a small vocal PA, keyboard and amp. Compact, for light planes and jeeps. A roadie with the package. Fella called Rob.

'Ten by road,' said Rob, but just two hours via the Cessna 402 we took to Tennant Creek. The gig, like all on this tour, at a First Nations community. Whitefellas needed permits. Jeeps with drivers at the airstrip.

'Play the room, Peter. Always play the room,' Robyn's maxim. Out here, that meant Jimmie Rodgers' *Waiting For A Train*, Hank's *Hey Good Lookin'*, Patsy's *Walking After Midnight*, and a yodelling turn. 'Mum taught me. Part of her schtick'.

And then we brought the house down. Well, the servo forecourt anyway, our stage that night. Slim never did *The Pub With No Beer* this way.

The caff there told me what Robyn already knew. The jukebox, Slim Dusty. Little else.

'Oh, about thirty beers,' from Rob when I asked. Gove from Darwin, Territory distance geometry, a longneck per hour by road. For us, just two frosties over Arnhem Land, bouncing around in a Beechcraft Bonanza eight seater. Jeeps the rest, to Yirrkala, then to Nhulumby. Here, Gamatj clan, Yolngu Nation. The legendary Yunupingu.

'Don't like the look of this.' No one had told us. Today, sorry business. A funeral, Galarrwuy Yunupingu's father. Grief and commitments as son and elder, yet gave us a pile of his time on the worst day of his life.

The gig, well. The gear stayed in the jeeps. The women keening, as per custom. I felt ashamed at being lost for words that might becalm, while Robyn and Garrulwuy went off for a heart to heart down by the jetty there. I hung back, ensorcelled, absorbing this place, a people part of its biosphere, its *soul,* from times past as infinite as the years to come.

Then joined them, for the soothing music of the sea. We didn't stay long. Wrong to linger. *We had no business being here.* A day that burned a brand on our spirits.

Groote Eylandt. Dutch, for 'Great Island.' For centuries the Anindilyakwa here had traded trepang, those gelatinous beasties of the shallows, with the city of Macassar, Sulawesi in Indonesia. Another Cessna to the airstrip. More jeeps to township Alyangula. The café, a jukebox. Yep, Slim Dusty. All of it.

Our stage that night, the tray of a truck. Mob here returned all the love we gave and so much more. For me, transformative, this week in a world I had so much more to learn about. This world of a force that refuses to be destroyed.

Back home, my universe was shrinking. Solo gigs fewer now with the passing of the piano bar goldrush. Just the Old Lion cellars now and again, or the City, my mainstay, the only late, late, late show in town. Here, the rampant Cold Chisel rolled in one night, Barnesy and Mossy joining me for a ripup of *Georgia On My Mind.* The Angels another time, with old comrade Chris B.

The City, a favoured lesbian, gay and trans hang, such venues in the shadows then. As a rule, they only opened round midnight, right after the yobs had been turfed out of the pubs. So the City hired heavy doormen, boxers and prizefighters, it was said, out of dire need, to enforce *no pasaran* to bash-happy gangs of the pissed and punchy. Not a night went by...

The entire upstairs floor above the Mediterranean, or so the scuttle went, the domain of a sex slave cartel. Off limits, of course, and I'm not about to try and find out. And Adelaide's after midnight non-hetero nightlife, the whispers on the wind, the empire of one Don Storen, who also ran the Med, in cahoots with silent partners invisible, big league and mean. They took a piece of your off the grid clubs like ACDC on Currie Street, or at the Colonel Light Hotel, it was reported, in return for their protection.

A boxing promoter as well, Don. Given the rumours, a good fit for a game fixed and crook. And most likely zero connection, but this was a time of unsolved child abductions and grisly slayings round our town, held by the nation for decades afterwards to be some kind of sex murder hellhub.

Locals took to speculating. The concept of *The Family* took hold, an imagined cult of local politicians, cops, property tycoons, barristers, judges, *all in on it*, the paranoid concoction of a frightened city trying to make sense of this loathsome unknown.

So at the City and 'neath the throb of the Lion Disco, the kitchens' clatter, the hiss of country killed steak, that year of '79, I played on for crumbs from tables of swine. Bare sufficient to stay, not nearly enough to leave. Stranded.

Like Robinson Caruso.

FIFTY-FOUR

It had to happen. Lit good and proper off an allnighter at the City, I come to at the wheel just in time to swerve from the parked cars in my path, and near clobber the cops come up alongside.
'Fuck me. Double figures. You should be dead, son.' Bag turned green. 'You can fucking walk home, party boy.'

Mouse went back to drive the wagon home. 'Exy', all I could say of my day in court. License suspended, nine months. Fine, two notes shy of five Cs. But the shame, the guilt, beyond calculation.

So I decided. No more driving, not ever. The magistrate, in tones of frostbite, had suggested just that, and I took it as wise counsel. From here on, *I, solus*. No bands, no gear, just me and inhouse pianos, all gigs close to home. It gave me fresh cause to return now, body and soul, to a place that bid again and again in the long watches of the night that I so do.

Out on that frequency only crims and musos can hear, I heard the Cross call my name.

'Peter, is it?'
'Yeah. Um, wh....'
'Peter Farrell here.' From the *News*. Wanted to do a piece on me. He'd been hipped to the Bon Scott connection, Robyn A, the Rangers, Headband. His story spoke of my 'eyes screwed up against the daylight'. To journos, we night people, part bat. Or vampire. My story, the way Farrell wrote it up, 'a catalogue of broken dreams.'

Well, I told it like it am. And so he did paint it, *his bitterness not for the system which has excluded him from stardom, but...which makes artists compromise their ideals to survive.*

Yeah. Close enough for jazz.

The shooter from the *News* took a pic. At the Lion's piano, glancing up like a crook at a hitman come for his life, in my Frank Booth *one suave fuck* look. Jacket, skivvy, white scarf. Farrell wrote of Woody High, of me as an 'eyes-aglow fifteen year old.' *Aglow*. I peered into a Jim Beam mirror at the Lion. Where had *that* gone?

'You want to *what?*' Farrell called again a week on.

'I see a major talent who just needs a bit of profile, Peter.' He'd *manage* me, he said. Well, he knew my world. And a journo, so players with shows to sell took his calls. Didn't dare not to. Yet he never got me a single gig. Maybe didn't know that's what a manager does. But wrote me up in *The News,* over and again. A skeptic might say I'd slung him a dip. I hadn't. My income didn't run to bribes. In fact, he took no fee. And my own phone started to ring off all this gratis promo. But best of all, he went in hard on late payers. Couldn't abide it.

'Owes me for six weeks worth now.' The way the wind told it, Storen used to blow the takings from his venues on cocaine and rent boys, a lot of one and more than that of the other. And Don's bruisers from the fight game hovered in his shadow, vibes that seethed. But the Don hadn't bargained on Fearless Farrell.

'Fuck him.' Farrell stomped up to the City, a block up from the News Ltd building, and dropped a load of weapons-grade standover on the Don. Storen's venues needed good press, the guts of it. The Fazz wants my cash, pronto, or see what happens.

'Tell you what,' says the Don. 'A cheque, made out to cash. Bank's across the street. You can take it over there right now.'

'I see his game three miles off,' Farrell said later. 'But don't want you to lose your gig, so *fair enough*, I say. It's right on closing time, so I sprint across. They refuse me outright. Our Don, bad debts all over.'

Back at the City, Farrell scrunched up the cheque, flung it at Storen, all righteous fury at being played, dead lucky Don's punch-drunk palookas not on deck at that time of day. Then sees Storen looking past him, alarmed, at these two joes in overalls. They've schlepped in the back way, unscrewed the legs off the baby grand, and now wheeling it out. *Repo.*

Storen freaked. Begged them to hang on, jumped on the blower to someone. Made for the till, scooped out a fistful of cash. Laid this on the repo men, who shrugged and trundled it back in.

'So, Don,' says Farrell. 'While you're at it,...' My hero. Wish we'd met long, long ago.

It was that long hot week that stretches and yawns between Xmas and New Year. Those last months of '79, I'm adrift, Mouse and I separated again, me never much of a sailor on the choppy seas that parental obligations blow your way. But I soon found a rental close by. Two doors down from the fam, as it happened. Enough rooms that housemate Freddy Hampton and I set up a studio.

'Peter! How would you be?' He's home between ACDC swings across Europe, the US, Australia. Just one night in town, en route to Freo and family there. Then London, to the next tour, and all the next.

Bon's holding a bottle of Jack D or maybe it was Jim B. Me, some Northern Rivers best bud. He's not himself, down and lost, was the word round town. He did come across a trifle rageworn when he rocked up that night. But my take, much of that down to non-stop touring, sleep deprivation, the smorgasbord of road sex, not some deeper dweller, albeit he came across as more reflective than usual.

'Yeah, too bad it went that way,' Bon's blue notes of regret. 'I owe her some financial support. Need to sort that out.' They'd just caught up in Melbourne. Still friends, he said, testament to Irene's big heart.

But he talked happy too, of touring. Of cowtowns conquered across Texas, Georgia, Alabama, as well as the Old Euro cities of Belgium and Germany. 'I don't know which is more weird.' And of his pay rise, first in five years with the Seedies. As for tonight, he couldn't wait to get out on the streets. 'Must be a show on somewhere.' But *better fix our heads first,* he said. Good and wired, we headed out on foot.

'Here we go, Peter. What did I tell ya?' A party, spilling out on to the street. Bon, quite the profile now, ACDC, regulars on the ABC's *Countdown*, radio, non-stop. *Highway To Hell, High Voltage, Dirty Deeds.*

We're crashers, but they're stoked to see Bon. His easy *G'day*, served with smile and chuckle, the most charming thing I ever saw. That and his habit of widening his eyes and sticking his tongue out of a grin, when good clean filthy fun loomed. *How about this, eh?*

Didn't take long. Two women attached themselves to us. Well, to Bon. Took us upstairs.

'Better hit the frog and toad. Plane to catch.' Not quite sunup as Bon bids us goodbye. 'Till next time, then.'

But old mate kismet, other plans. I miss him every day.

FIFTY-FIVE

'Oh, the usual. Out on a job last night,' they said. First day here, the coffee shop opposite the pub I'd be playing. They spot the out-of-towner right off. But friendly. A few Qs, where I'm from, why I'm here. They're in town to re-stock on ammo, they say. Their line of work, *spotlighting*, they said. I knew what that was.

'Oh, yeah. Roos or pigs?'

'No, mate.' Both sniggered. 'The c..ns,' said one.

'Yeah.' The other. 'The b...gs. Lonely, dirty work, but someone's gotta do it.' Laughing as they said it. Louder as I stood up and walked out.

Alice Springs, aswarm with tourists, to see how *traditional* people live. A con they're sold. The souvenir shops, all plastic boomerangs, stuffed koalas and tea towels, from third world sweatshops offshore, emblazoned with stolen art and motifs. *Gammin.* Fake, cheap and nasty.

And so-called *art galleries,* posters of Namatjira paintings, batik prints. Yet the bark art of Wandjina stories, real enough, made by locals, ten bucks a pop. I bought half a doz across my two months there. Eerie images. I'd heard that mob can be mischievous, making up tales for gullible gubbas. But asked anyway.

'Oh, that's the sky people. From our Dreamtime.' I'm a rube stayed too long at the carny maybe, but full-on intrigued. *Sky people.* Other days, they called them *cloud people. Star people.*

'To me,' I said one day, 'they look like aliens.' Next I knew, they're telling me more.

'This mob, from the Pleiades, bud,' one of the nearest star clusters to Earth. Sure, maybe they saw me coming. Pressed further, they declared it *secret business,* not for gubs to be asking.

Fair enough. But it lined up with what I saw. These were beings not of this world.

And amidst this tat and chintz, the 'real story' the mugs had come for yet chose to ignore, right before their eyes, the poisoned fruit of dispossession. Blackfellas drinking in clusters on the streets. Some paralytic, passed out, or swearing abuse at all comers, hard and loud. No bloody wonder. The pale dorks pass them by, eyes aswerve. They're invisible.

'I volunteered. To keep the bashers in line.' Here, a frontier forever war. Cops, out and proud racist. The one exception, a sergeant, young guy. Ex-junkie, he let slip one day. On his watch, he put a collar and a leash on his constables. 'So a little more peace, a little less war.'

The Alice, one of *those* towns. Everyone's from somewhere else, on the drift or on the run. Ron T, managing the Uluru Motel, tipped me off. A gig going, the Riverside Hotel's new piano bar. To pull tourists, and local free-spending hoons. Blackfellas, more or less barred. Charlie Perkins, the civil rights legend, came in one night, but with whitefella escort from the Minister's department.

Down the street at the Great Northern, a blackfellas only bar out the back. But most of them drank down on the Todd River bank. Not barred there. Yet.

There was one young fella they let in the piano bar. Dressed white, talked the gubba talk. Had a job, novel for mob here. Name of Charlie. We bonded fast. Drugs. From Charlie, a new one on me. *Pituri*. Bush opium. Lays you out, high as the Himalayas.

'Let's do it'. Charlie, myself and Linda, a regular at the bar, pooled our stashes one day. Acid, yarndi, pituri. A five hour drive to Uluru from the Alice, on my only day off, so we jumped on a turboprop 44 seater Fokker Friendship with other whitefella pilgrims.

Yeah, we were full ripped and flashing, but it was no excuse. And Charlie, a Pitjantjatjara man, knew naught of the *taboo*. At the Rock, we stayed hours topside after the climb, too gone to move, befouling a sacred site. May Kurpany the devil dog strike me down.

Piano bar at the Riverside, not the only show in town. At the Great Northern up the street, Ted Egan. Ted wrote *Gurindji Blues* with Gurindji man Vincent Lingiari in 1969, he of the Wave Hill stockmen's strike. It was Lingiari into whose hand Gough Whitlam poured the soil of his land, in symbolic handback to its real owners.

Ted didn't play guitar. Instead, an empty slab carton, a Fosterphone or a VBphone depending on what it had housed. Slim Dusty? Well, Slim is great, but he ain't Ted. And if you don't get Ted, you just don't get it.

Like most Australians, I knew zero of Indigenous cultures. My dad Len had branded them all *dirty, smelly drunks,* and to *stay away from them.* Yet if not for that, I'd never have gone questing to know more. *What did they know that we didn't?*

Well. Take sixty millennia of cosmology, agriculture, botany, biology, chemistry, physics, zoology, medicine, land, fire and water management, from just shy of three hundred Nations.

How long you got?

FIFTY-SIX

I wanted to pack and sail for Sydney the day I rolled back from the Alice, but came offers now no destitute muso could refuse.

'Peter. Busy?' CBA calling. 'Piano player's crook.' The gig, tonight. Full house. So it's climb into a suit, barrel in to Festi Theatre and catch in mid-air the charts tossed my way, ten minutes to showtime. But Charley couldn't thank me enough. Mr Pride made me feel like I was the star here. The band, hot. Got tight with me, a blow-in stabbing in the dark, as if I'd been out on the boards with these smokin' guns for a thousand nights.

'Can you go in *now?*' Around a week after that, woken by the phone at midday. Big name, sellout show. Rehearse all arv, then gig right after that, at Festi Theatre. Tonight. Not a piano job this time. I'd just bought a Solina string synth, for the studio with Fred. 'Oh, and bring that gizmo with ya.'

Killer band, some of Sydney's hotmost. Twelve pieces, but no string section. Strange, to be skimping on the fiddles and bows so integral to this brand of blockbuster schmaltz. Their asking price perhaps more than Kamahl thought his fans deserved.

'Here's your charts.' *Thirty songs.* The string parts, said the MD. 'Just wing it, maestro. You'll be right.'

'Stop. Stop. Everybody, stop, please!' An hour into rehearsal, the star calls cut, midsong. *Oh fuck,* thinks me. *He knows I'm bluffing. I'm history.* 'These,' he says to the stage manager, pointing at each in turn, the little red pilot lights on our amps. 'Can't you turn them off?'

The stage crew here had seen it all, survived battalions of prima donnas. Matter of minutes, they've broken out the gaffa tape and taped twenty-cent pieces over every one. The Big K abides no lights save those shone upon him. One weird day's journey into night.

'Sure. When do we leave?' *A Star Is Torn*, back on the road.
'That's great, Peter. Album's out, you see. Need to plug this baby far and wide.'
'Album?'
'Yeah. Of the show.' Turned out that Robyn had tracked the *Star* show at Sydney's Trafalgar studio while I'd been in the Alice. The producer, Tony Ansell, played on the sesh. Fair call. I wasn't around. Yet more reason, I reminded myself, to fold your tent in our little town and *get where the action is.*

Rehearsals before a run at The Space at Adelaide's Festi Theatre. Then, five weeks, York Theatre, Seymour Centre, Sydney. 'Ready to fight and die for Billie, Patsy and Janis, Peter?' Robert Gavin, replaced as the other pianist by a ballet and opera first call go-to, Dale Ringland. We kicked off the day after Anzac Day,1980. All May, half of June. Sydney loved Robyn and she loved back.

'Oh, come on, Peter. Live a little large.' Robyn had an itch for Sydney nightlife, Oxford St Darlinghurst style. Post-show, any night of the week, we'd make for the 'Golden Mile' as they called it. Robyn, worshipped here as if the goddess Lakshimi. We were near swamped in free champagne where'er we roved.

A joint called Pinocchio's was Robyn's go-to, my eyes out on bedsprings at just how down and dirty the show was. All naked or as good as, a conga line of young fellas, er, conjoined at the rear as they rhumboogied through the crowd.

'Some day I'll fly away...' At the Exchange and the Albury, drag shows. The outfits these divas rocked, full dazzling, but my inner musician didn't dig on the fact that none of them sang, all of them miming to records. But down to Robyn's divine status hereabouts, I'm

awash in free rivers of gold medal grog, so not mine to grumble. I think we made the scene at Patches and Flo's Palace as well, but any memory of either lie as skeletons on the floor of the Sea Of Dom Perignon.

He had a terrace house in Underwood St, Paddo. A spare room there, mine for free. 'Long as you like,' he said when I'd called to tee up a catchup. Vince Lovegrove had bounced between Melbourne and here for the last few years, as a journo for *A Current Affair*, then a producer on the *Don Lane Show* until the night he booked a touring Tom Waits for an interview with Don. Vince rendered unto Waits all the hospitality that the green room fridge could hold, and in the wake of the shambles resulting, was bounced from the show for evermore the next day. Managing Cold Chisel now, so here he be.

And along with Vince and girlfriend Daina, but seldom seen, Jimmy Barnes lived here. The band, shaping a new album close by in Woolloomooloo, at a new setup called Paradise Studios.

'Wanna stroll down for a sticky?' Chisel had the joint block-booked twenty-four seven, 'a lockout,' said Vince, 'for access whatever the hour, should inspiration strike.' I've just rocked in, *Star* done for the night, and it's whatever o'clock as it happened. 'Fun city down there.'

'Ain't called 'Paradise' for nothing,' said Vince. Most studios, Soviet-grade utilitarian, but here, a spa, a snooker and billiards room, pinball machines, and abrim to the gunwales with Chisel's choice of finest French, platoons of those Bourbons of Kentucky, single malts, exotic liqueurs. Ned Kelly's 'conscience as clear as the snow in Peru' came to mind when I beheld there a hillside of the stuff. Smoko likewise. Vince waved his hand across it all. 'Whatever gets you through the night.'

'Peter!' He gripped my forearm and hand with both of his, yanked me in close, Bob Hawke style. 'Vince tells me you're absolutely marvellous!' He'd played bars around Sydney for some years and had set up Paradise about a year back. It was here I first met Billy Field. 'It's been brought to my attention that we're of the same feather.' He'd played bass or guitar in bands, but now, piano, originals as a solo. 'It's no task for flakes, brother.'

Billy, a thing for jazz and swing. 'It's my contention that you could still bust the charts asunder with a big band swing number. Never gets old, that gear,' he said. And did just that a year on with *Bad Habits*. We got pretty tight as time rolled on. Bill, full of great tips and contacts round the scene. A special kind of diamond, that one.

'Well, Chisel have done a pile of shows at jails of late, so it's come to inform some of the new songs,' he said in that drawl in no rush to be anyplace, forged as a kid up in FNQ and later Grafton. 'That and all this,' pointing his Danneman cigar at the whirlwind about us, Baron's on Roslyn St up the Cross, its chesterfield lounges, backgammon tables and bar open all night. Don Walker lived close by to Baron's, itself opposite Les Girls. On the nights I wasn't out with Robyn or with Vince down at Paradise, I'd go a-roving solo round the Cross. Scoping it out for gigs, maybe even a place to live, for when I made the move. I'd often run into Don in the course of these trawls, at Baron's or the down at heel All Nations Club on Bayswater Road or a gone to seed pub, the Pilsener Inn, once at a total sleazehole called the Barrell Inn. A true nocturnal, Don, and a taste for the seamy as preferred bars went. Brilliant mind, but quiet, reserved, a deep blue and rakish brand of humour.

Ground zero KX come 1980, Darlinghurst Rd, the 'dirty half mile' and all its multitudes of toilers on the game. A shoal of adult bookstores, Club X and such. Porno out now on VHS and Beta, but here still, X-rated cinemas alongside 'erotic boutiques' touting lingerie, fetishwear for all reasons and seasons.

And strip clubs galore, spruikers out front all bow ties, short sleeved white shirts, all the better to swing a fist, shouting over the traffic of *knickers, knackers and the old piss flappers*. Within, not just dancers, but live sex shows, glory holes, or, it was said, power drinking contests onstage, the winner rewarded with a dancer of choice.

The Summary Offences Act repealed in recent time, so cops couldn't bust street sex workers for vagrancy or loitering any more. The streets, aswarm with starters. And despite it still being illegal, brothels like the Nevada, its signage promoting *Australia's Largest Bed,* flaunted their presence loud and painted brazen. Street preachers yapped of the hell awaiting the sinners who dodged around them. These holy rollers, the same king rat look about them as their targets. They never had a chance.

And the Cross had supermarkets, banks, takeaway food joints and milk bars too, but in the swirl of all that other, these all looked as if they'd got lost on the way to somewhere else. 'Yep,' said Don one night, 'there's no place like home.'

It was all very entertaining as I poked around the X, convinced now that *I could make a real career here*. Bars and clubs with jazz trios and quartets, blues bands or piano players flourished amid all that sex for sale. The Bourbon and Beefsteak, perfect for my schtick. The Regency Room at the Hyatt Kingsgate, a grand piano, jazz trios, or the Paradise Jazz Cellar on Darlinghurst Rd. And other joints, piano bars or jazzpits that would come to be called Round Midnight, Illusions, and a revived El Rocco club in the days to come.

Beyond the Cross, live music all nights of the week. A good slice of it, jazz. The storied Basement on Reiby Place in the city, Jenny's on Goulburn St, Backstage and Soup Plus on George St, the Marble Bar at the Sydney Hilton, the Musicians Club, Surry Hills. Here I saw beckoning, a forever refuge and a thousand nights of glory.

'It's finished, lads. Wanna have a listen?' Jimmy barrelled through the door, chucked it on and cranked it loud. The quiet one in the plan this night, just Vince, a spliff and me, swept aside by Cyclone Chisel. Some hours on, we're singing, well, howling along to the tenth time round for *Cheap Wine, Choir Girl, Rising Sun*, the birds of dawn silenced by the jewel that was the newborn *East*. A killer finish to a cathartic five weeks in Sydney Town. I couldn't wait to get back, next time for good.

Star, due up north now, two weeks at Her Maj. Accom, four-star motel, only safe refuge from Brisneyland cops for a quiet choof. Hayseed tyrant Joh Bjelke-Petersen, Premier now since '68. At the time, it felt like he'd be there till the last clock at the oldest end of the universe ticked no more.

Back in Adelaide, a week of *Star*. From there, the Octagon Theatre, Perth. On the plane west, the ground below rolled by, immemorial as time.

'You up for it, Peter?' Was I ever. Three weeks now, Melbourne, the Comedy Theatre. And news. Brit impresario Helen Montagu had seen *Star*. Keen to give it a run in the West End. Top of that, Alan Carr, producer of the Village People flick *Can't Stop The Music,* blown clear out of his caftan, and talking large of an off-Broadway staging.

'We could be away for a year. More if I can help it,' said Robyn. *London. New York.* Robyn going global. *Forget Sydney, Peter.* A new dreamscape I beheld. My own gigs clubside. Ronnie Scott's, the Blue Note, Birdland. The stars, close enough to reach out and touch.

Hold that plane.

'Sorry, chum.' New York, no go, says Robyn. Fell through. And London, well. 'It's the Brit unions. Pommy players only.'

Well, there went that. Skint again. The City and those other gigs had folded, so I had to go back on the dragnet. At a joint just opened, Lark And Tina's, at first, just me, on late after the main band, but I took to doing duos, with Mauri B or Philby.

'Let's call it Fred And The Head,' he said. Fred Hampton, partner in those schmoodles of jingles at Slater's, had a jones to work live again. He snagged a gig at the Inn On The Park, east end of Rundle Street, the old city market precinct. Now, all head shops, vego restaurants, the Hambly-Clark gun store, its signage howling *Toys For Men,* and Marxist bookstores. Yep. Something for everyone.

At our studio, me back now with Mouse and kids two doors up, Fred and I did jingles, demo sessions, all that he could reap of the scant crop to be had. To make the rent, we gave ABC radio and TV *Rocturnal* presenter Dave Woodhall a room here now, and Vytas Serelis another. It was some scene. The four stoners of the Rockalypse. When came a stranger with even stranger news.

It was Adelaide Festival time again. On the job at the Festi Theatre piano bar, and in rolls a tiger woman in red and gold. This friend of hers, she said, the manager of the Beverly Plaza Hotel. Three months, the job, a work visa for Taiwan only good for that, and an emperor's treasure for my trouble.

'Leave it with me, Mr Head.' Farrell did the rest. They wanted PR pix, so he lined up a shooter and a tux, white, floor to ceiling. 'Client's request.' Me, not about to argue. The nut's two large a week and I'm broke as North Korea.

'Mr Peter! Welcome to Taipei! So delighted, sir!' Not Chinese, Mr Baba. Straight outta Jakarta, if I had to take a stab. A hassle at Kai Tak airport in Hong Kong en route. *Name different from passport,* they said. 'Peter Head' on the ticket, but *mon passeport* still says Beagley. Nearly missed the connecting flight. But at Chiang kai-Shek International, waved straight through, our driver right out front of the terminal. My man Baba, it was plain, a dude connected. To the Beverly Plaza, the *Bevvy* to Western expats, in a long white Ford LTD.

The said Bevvy, five-star. They flip me the key to a suite pushing seven. But first to business. 'Mr Peter, come with me, please.' The elevator sailed us in silent majesty down to the basement. 'Here you play, maestro,' beams Mr Baba. *A giant room, empty. Air with walls.* 'What piano would you like?' *It's Asia. Haggle. Start way over the top.*
   'Um...I like Steinways. A concert grand if...'
   'Very good, sir.' *Fuck. Too easy.* 'And where?' It's a basement, so the only windows, up high on one wall.
   'How about over ther...' I'm dazed. I manage half an answer, in a minor key.
   'Splendid.' He jumped on the phone. No English now. Tone, same in any lingo. Giving orders. Ten minutes go by. We talk set times, breaks, repertoire. I nod, smile, to mask my rising concern. This gig, the stench of a dud. *Have I been played?*

Then out of nowhere, I swear, fifty workers. Up went bamboo scaffolding. *Bamboo.* They're scrambling all over it now. Some of them, barefoot. Ants on speed.

Three days on, those ants have knocked up a max luxed-up bar, *the* hot spot for Taiwan's A-listers. Film stars, singers, the president, and those billionaire crims to whom all such, in all far flungs of the globe, are beholden.

I sang Billy Joel, to pre-empt request stalkers and other potential hostiles. Elton John, same strategy. Plus my speciality, singers untroubled by vocal virtuosity. Randy Newman or Tom Waits, his early stuff, before he went all Captain Beefheart smog monster. Patrons here, mostpart Taiwanese and Hong Kong tycoons. Their trophy squeezes, all silk, diamonds, pearls. Not all Chinese. High-rolling Thais, South Koreans, Japanese, Filipinos and Filipinas.

The brass from the US bases here, a disappointment. No US Cavalry hats, corncob pipes, not one eyepatch. Ken dolls in dress blues, heads by *Thunderbirds*. Of the foreign diplomats, I amused myself deducing which ones were the spooks. Yep. The gods drank here. The food, ambrosial. And for those fearful of spice in their lives, Western menu as well as pan-Asian. Yankee not adventurous in matters chowdown.

'Ah, Mr Petah. Very famous,' guests were saying. *Eh?* Then I picked up a *South China Morning Post* in the foyer. *There I was.* Giant ad, front page, that pic snapped back in Adelaide. Broadcast out loud that I was *gweilo, lao wai,* a longnose paleface. A comfort to the Yanks, a novelty for the local quality. They ran it daily for months. Nutsville. I Was A Taiwanese Pop Star. Then all too soon, it was time to go home.

FIFTY-SEVEN

Trooping off the plane across that windburned tarmac of my lifetime home, it hit me amidships, as it always did these days, that plunging mood swing. I was done here. Or it was done with me. I'd saved enough off that Taiwan job to make it happen. About to break it to Mouse, *now is the hour,* when the phone rang.

'National tour, Peter.' Diana, Robyn's manager. 'Two solo shows. One of Brecht songs. The other, well, that's where you come in.'

Robyn Archer At Large, an evening of jazz and country classics. Myself plus Louis McManus, of late with the Bushwhackers, a hot hand on guitar, mandolin, fiddle. *One Take McManus,* record producer Tony Cohen called him. For sax and flute, Don Reid. A pedigree of dazzle, Don, late of Rory O'Donoghue's Cool Bananas and the Daly Wilson Big Band.

'Oh, one other thing.' After *Large,* a run of *Star* in Sydney. 'Would you be...?'

At Large, first run, the Sydney Festi of '82. Robyn's Brecht show with others, back to back nights with ours. Goes and goes, that Robyn, like a runaway train.

'What fresh hell is *this?*' We're playing the big room, but the wrong one. There'd been talk of staging Robyn's shows at the smaller spaces at the Opera House, a schmick fit for cabaret turns. But demand for tickets such that they plonked us down in that glorified Hindenburg hangar, Sydney Town Hall. Room sound, a quagmire of echoes, Robyn unintelligible to the thousands crammed in there each night.

Not all bad for me. The Bosendorfer concert grand here, a *beast*. Three extra bass keys at the extreme left of the keyboard. The stage shook when I played 'em. I found fresh reasons to go there every night.

For the Sydney run this go-round, I crashed at a house Robyn owned in Petersham with partner and manager Diana. Weird joint. David Lynch qualities. Once six bedsits, a boarding house, and they hadn't changed it any. At some point, I had to move out. Why, long gone from memory, perished at its perimeter. But Robyn saw me right, phoned a friend. Penny Chapman, a movie producer, took me in. My crib, the attic of a terrace in a Darlo side street, where those last lingering misgivings of my plan to return here faded to black. *This was where I belonged.*

'Home ground advantage, comrade.' *At Large* now to Adelaide, its Town Hall. No need for Robyn to *prove it* here. They'd known her since the beginning of forever. On to the Golden West, Perth Concert Hall for that city's Arts Festi. Then across that stretch boundless between Indian and Pacific, for a run in Melbourne. To wind up, the first days of March '82, Brisbane, Her Maj. Our last night there, Louis aflame on guitar and fiddle as Robyn brought down the whole damn town.

And so to home. But not for long. *At Large*, the last I played before I said *see ya* to where I'd lived near all my days, Mouse and kids to follow me to our new place in the world. I packed a go-bag, lined up a piece of floor to flop for the Sydney run of *Star* and a fistful of side gigs that Robyn's teed up. A brand new nightclub, she said. Ex-funeral parlour, name of Kinselas.

Away now, like Bon, on the only ticket to ride. One way.

AFTERWORD

None of this story would have been possible without the contributions of the following, and my heartfelt thanks to all of them.

To Dave Woodhall and his suggestion for the title.

To Robert Beagley, Mauri Berg, Joff Bateman, Johnny Mac, Marlene Richards, Bev Harrell, Loene Furler, Shirley Smith, Tony Martino, Alex Innocenti, Victor Marshall, Rob George, Brenda Maxwell, Freddy Payne, Geoff Kluke, Joey Moore, Geoff O'Connor, Paul Goodwin, Richard Ivey, John Howell, Bob Lott, Electric Nick, John Bywaters, Paul Hille, Greg Rosman, Gene Pierson, Phil Colson, Lee Cass, Robyn Archer, Doug Ashdown, Max Pepper, Rick Kent, 'Spook' Spencer, John McGregor, Peter McCormack, Rob Tillett, Grahame Conlon, Peter Farrell, Lucky Starr and Bobby Bright for sharing their memories and recollections.

To Vytas Serelis and Ron Tremaine for being there.

And R.I.P. Wendy Saddington, Jeff St. John, Bon Scott, Phil Wooding, Chris Bailey, Bruce Howe, Brian Porter, Dave Colvill, Ray Arnold, Boz Burrell, Mick Jurd, Jim Keays, Roger Frampton, Jimmy Little, Frankie Davidson, Vince Lovegrove and Sybil Graham.

I look forward to making music again with you again soon in the Big Band Blow in the sky, but first I've got to write the sequel to this bloody book.

Peter Head

www.ingramcontent.com/pod-product-compliance
Lightning Source LLC
Chambersburg PA
CBHW050106170426
43198CB00014B/2482